Praise for
I Hope So

"Hope is the most underrated performance enhancer on the planet. Every chapter of this book is packed with wisdom and tools you can use immediately—in the locker room, the boardroom, and the living room!"

ALAN STEIN JR., keynote speaker and author of *Raise Your Game*

"This book lit a fire in me when I needed it most. I now see hope not as passive but as power."

NATALIE TYSDAL, health journalist and host of *The Natalie Tysdal Podcast*

"*I Hope So* is like a deep breath for your soul. It's packed with simple, practical ways to build hope, and it just makes life feel a little lighter."

STU MCLAREN, cofounder of Membership.io

"Dr. Robyne has written a book that is a shining beacon of hope for a very dark world."

DR. GREG WELLS, author of *The Ripple Effect*, *Powerhouse*, and *Superbodies*

"*I Hope So* shows us how we can develop a grounded hope practice that fills the many facets of our lives so we can operate with more courage, face the unknown with grace, and believe wholeheartedly in possibility."

PHYLICIA GEORGE, 3x Olympian and Olympic medalist

"Dr. Robyne delivers a how-to guide addressing our greatest need right now: hope. Most importantly, she offers strategy, applicability, relevance, and a lovingly illuminated path toward cultivating it."

PETER KATZ, Juno Award–nominated singer-songwriter and facilitator

"Whether you are asking for your own heart-centered evolution or to lead a soul-centered global revolution, Dr. Robyne will inspire and elevate your belief in the power and purpose of hope."

DR. JAMES ROUSE, Emmy Award–winning producer and founder of Optimum Wellness Media

"If you have HOPE, you're well on your way to better mental health. Dr. Robyne is the perfect guide for this journey."

KEVIN FRANKISH, mental health advocate

"In her characteristic warm voice, Dr. Robyne shows us that hope is not passive optimism or something we have to wish for, but a cultivable resource we can choose and share. *I Hope So* is a light in the dark."

SANDY COHEN, MPH, health journalist

"This book is a lifeline for anyone seeking resilience, meaning, and connection in an increasingly uncertain world. It's not just a book—it's a movement."

DEANNA BASSO, corporate event planner

"Dr. Robyne doesn't sugarcoat life's struggles, and that's why this book shines. It shows us that hope is not wishful thinking, but a strategy we can all choose."

LOREN LAHAV, founder of Stay True Creative Productions, executive coach, international keynote speaker, and leadership mentor

"Dr. Robyne balances research, personal stories, and just the right amount of humor to show that hope isn't only for optimists—it's for realists who want to keep going, grow stronger, and help others do the same."

JEN BENNETT, director of strategic initiatives at Bank of Montreal

"*I Hope So* is a beautifully written reminder that hope isn't naive—it's necessary. Dr. Robyne shows us how to hold on to possibility even in our hardest seasons and transform it into action."

MARISSA TEETER, executive coach and podcast host of *Teeter Talks*

"This book is a beautiful reminder that hope is not about denying reality, but about learning to coexist with what is while still believing in what can be."

PETRA KOLBER, author of *The Perfection Detox*, speaker, and DJ

"Dr. Robyne invites us to rediscover hope as a daily, intentional practice for thriving in uncertain times. When the world feels heavy, this is the book you'll return to for perspective, comfort, and above all, hope."

PAULA FELPS, podcast host of *Live Happy Now*

"*I Hope So* is an essential resource for those striving to enhance their well-being through the practice of hope-infused living. This book has provided me with precisely the inspiration I needed today."

STEPHEN BOBKO, transformational HR and business leader

"Dr. Robyne breaks down the complex into a simple concept on how to build resiliency, even when it's hard. As a business leader, I truly believe choosing a positive, hopeful mindset is key to inspiring others to be their best."
MARJOLAINE HUDON, financial sector senior executive

"With honesty and warmth, Dr. Robyne reminds us that hope is a choice and when we choose it, we find the strength to be present for our families, our friendships, our teams, and ourselves to do the hard things that matter most."
JACKIE TIJERINA, nonprofit career coach

"For anyone ready to transform doubt into courage, this book is the spark that empowers you to choose possibility over paralysis—and bravely step forward with HOPE!"
CHANTAL MCNEILY, investment and wealth advisor; president and board chair of FuturFund

"Thank you, Dr. Robyne, for offering me a new tool, a fresh perspective, and yes... some genuine newfound hope."
DUSTAN WOODHOUSE, founder of BTBB Inc.

I Hope So

I Ho

ROBYNE HANLEY-DAFOE

•• PAGE TWO

**HOW TO CHOOSE
HOPE EVEN
WHEN IT'S HARD**

Copyright © 2026 by Dr. Robyne Hanley-Dafoe

All rights reserved. No part of this book may be reproduced, stored in a retrieval system or transmitted, in any form or by any means, without the prior written consent of the publisher or a license from The Canadian Copyright Licensing Agency (Access Copyright). For a copyright license, visit accesscopyright.ca or call toll free to 1-800-893-5777.

Some names and identifying details have been changed to protect the privacy of individuals.

This book is not intended as a substitute for the medical advice of physicians. The reader should regularly consult a physician in matters relating to their health and particularly with respect to any symptoms that may require diagnosis or medical attention.

Cataloguing in publication information is available from Library and Archives Canada.
ISBN 978-1-77458-679-2 (paperback)
ISBN 978-1-77458-678-5 (ebook)

Page Two
pagetwo.com

Page Two™ is a trademark owned by Page Two Strategies Inc., and is used under license by authorized licensees

Cover design by Fiona Lee
Interior design by Jennifer Lum
Printed and bound in Canada by Friesens
Distributed in Canada by Raincoast Books
Distributed in the US and internationally by Macmillan

26 27 28 29 30   5 4 3 2 1

drrobyne.ca

To Lesley, who hoped for me,
To Hunter, Ava, and Jaxson, whom I hope for,
And to Little Robyne, who found hope in the dark:
Hope endures.

I RESPECTFULLY ACKNOWLEDGE that this work was created on the treaty and traditional territory of the Michi Saagiig Anishinaabeg. As a settler on these lands, I offer my gratitude to the caretakers of this land—past, present, and future—and honor their deep and enduring connection to this place.

I recognize that we all hold ancestral knowledge. My roots, known to me, are anchored in the ancient Scottish Highlands of Atholl and the rugged shores of Cork, Ireland—lands of myth, resiliency, and song. Yet my footsteps now trace paths far from where my ancestors once stood. Here, on this land, I carry their legacy while honoring the stories and traditions that have shaped this place long before me. In walking this Earth so far from my origins, I accept the responsibility to listen deeply, learn humbly, and live with gratitude, knowing that my presence is part of an unfolding story far greater than my own.

I basically owe my
life to hope. The very least I can
do is write a book about it.

Contents

Introduction		**Let's Hope This Is Good** 1
	1	**Pandora's Death Jar and Robyne Thinking While Driving** 11
	2	**Hopscotching Through Hope's History** 27
	3	**The Costs of Hopelessness and the Need for a Samwise Gamgee** 47
	4	**Key Hope Theories and a Few Good News Stories** 65
	5	**Everyday Resiliency and the Hope Variable** 83
	6	**From Hope to Resiliency** 101
	7	**Stress Wisely with a Dose of Hope** 121

	8	**The Evolution of Hope Across Life's Seasons** *145*
	9	**The Hope Blocks Model: Building a Life Tethered with Hope** *167*
	10	**Mapping Your Hope Blocks** *195*
	11	**Gifting Hope to Others** *213*
	12	**Final Thoughts and a Parting Wish** *243*
Epilogue		**Do Self-Help Books Even Have Epilogues?** *251*
		Acknowledgments *259*
		Notes *265*

INTRODUCTION

Let's Hope This Is Good

> When you have lost hope,
> you have lost everything.
> And when you think all is lost,
> when all is dire and bleak,
> there is always hope.

PITTACUS LORE

LIFE IS SOMETIMES compared to a tapestry. On one side, a magnificent design showcases the richness and expanse of the lived experience. The alternate side presents a tangled web of threads, interwoven yet separate, that appear to be more of a mess than a masterpiece. We rarely look at the underside of the textile, yet it's this hidden layer that holds the majestic picture together. Of all the possible threads we can untether, this book is dedicated to one—precious, often overlooked, but very likely the key to holding the precarious fabric of our lives together. The small yet mighty through line that makes showing up in every facet of our lives possible: the thread of hope.

I'm often asked whether there's a single key to resiliency or genuine well-being. My answer is always to cultivate a hope practice. From my observations, hope is the crucial thread weaving through all aspects of a fulfilling life. It's the practice that consistently transforms outcomes and defies the odds. I've seen firsthand how those who embrace hope navigate life differently. Their ability to withstand stress is greater. Their ability to forge a comeback after adversity is swifter. And their capacity to be truly and deeply well sets them apart from the average person. Yet the forces behind hope's remarkable efficacy often defy conventional understanding.

This powerful undercurrent driving human behavior can seem full of contradictions. For instance, hope isn't technically an emotion; it's more of a full-body navigational system that points to the possibility of things somehow working out despite not knowing how. Unlike optimism, which is attached to a specific outcome, hope believes that everything will be all right *despite* the outcome. Hope is often described as a cognitive state or mindset, yet it's felt in the body; people tend to lean into the sensory experience of hope and the despair one feels when hope is absent. And hope impacts action. How many of us make New Year's resolutions year after year despite how quickly we statistically break them? Similarly, people end relationships hoping to find love again, even after heartbreak. After losing a beloved pet, many invite a new puppy into their lives, trusting in the healing power of unconditional love. From my own experience, I know that while my beloved chocolate lab Tycho wasn't with me for my whole life, she had me for every day of hers. And I continue to find hope in the knowledge that I loved her completely in our time together. Even when it seems to defy the odds, hope opens us up to new experiences, ultimately shaping our lives for the better.

Hope is also inherently polarizing. Two individuals in the same situation can hope for entirely different outcomes. The pitcher hopes to strike out the batter, while the batter hopes for a home run. A boyfriend hopes his girlfriend will accept his proposal, even as she might wish it were his best friend asking instead. In a conflict, each side hopes for victory. This raises questions about the moral dimensions of hope: Whose hope practice prevails in the end? Is one person's hope more worthy or good or deserved than another's?

Despite its generally positive connotations, hope can be complex and confusing. Some people seem to have an abundance of hope, while for others hope is fleeting. Some view hope as their greatest strength, while others see it as a weakness. Hope can also change shape over time into something we may not recognize.

I've witnessed a card-carrying atheist cry out to God to save his wife's life despite ridiculing other people for their faith. Hope often defies our own expectations and beliefs.

The same way hope can be vital to our well-being, a lack of hope can have grave consequences. For instance, a diagnosis of cancer leads to discussions about cure rates, treatment options, and quality of life. Conversely, rarely is hope mentioned during a mental health diagnosis. For most, a diagnosis of a mental health condition feels more like a life sentence, often met with stigma that discourages early intervention and support. People bring casseroles for cancer patients. The community rallies with optimism and care. In contrast, a mental health diagnosis can lead to isolation and judgment, with less community support and more blame directed at the individual or their families. Very few people diagnosed with a mental health condition receive casseroles. As a consequence, many delay seeking help until hope seems lost, exacerbating the crisis. Hope absolutely needs to be infused in seemingly hopeless situations.

Grounded in my research as an award-winning educational behavioralist and resiliency expert, this book will explore why hope ignites the most profound aspects of our being, and how we can harness it. Together, we'll dive deep into how hope motivates the wisest parts of us to live and be well, building the lifelong skill set that will help us navigate through it all.

Continuing the Conversation

In exploring other books about hope, I encountered a few common obstacles. Many books on hope tell amazing stories of people who navigated wildly difficult and even terrifying life events. I get it: "Despite the odds" stories have the power to be uplifting and inspirational. While I happen to have one or two of those stories myself, for some people, sensational stories don't inspire hope at all. Rather, they make hope seem reserved for a select few. Despite many stories having what might be considered a happy ending, the act of reading such heavy content leave some people feeling even more discouraged about the hardships and injustices in the world. I also found a central theme of trauma in many hope books, with the message that "if I can do it, so can you." It felt like some books about hope were leaving people behind.

Many books about hope are also quite siloed. Some delve into the hard science behind hope while perhaps dismissing the transcendent human experience that it can be. On the other hand, the vast collection of beautiful and awe-inspiring testimonies of "overcoming" seldom examine how that hope was possible, just that it happened. I found many record books where I was looking for a guidebook. Other books tend to be quite religious, which may leave those who struggle with faith or religious institutions feeling even more abandoned or unseen. While each of these approaches to exploring hope have their own important place, if I wanted to start an inclusive, practical "hope collective," a group of people willing to be hopefilled in a world shadowed in despair, I realized I needed to braid together as many distinct threads of hope as possible.

My aim is to create a body of work that speaks to as many people as possible, because hope ought to be a practice that unites, not divides or abandons. I want to help drive the movement that living hopefilled is both scientifically and spiritually sound! Is that even possible? I HOPE SO. I'm hoping you do too.

So, welcome to the new frontier of the human hope experience, dear reader. I'll present a blend of research—both quantitative and qualitative—to uncover hope's history, the cost of hopelessness, and the key hope variables, alongside inspiring and accessible stories of individuals and organizations who have embraced hopefilled living and working. From these insights, I'll present actionable strategies and practices that foster resiliency and well-being rooted in hope.

Many people aspire to be more hopeful in general. Some have mastered being hopeful most of the time. Few have honed the art and science of living hopefilled even during the worst of days. But that can be us. Together, we can and will transform hope from a concept into a powerful practice that radically transforms our lived experience, because the quality of our lives depends on it.

PS I'm so glad you're here with me. And I hope you find exactly what you need.

1
Pandora's Death Jar and Robyne Thinking While Driving

> Some people cannot see a good thing when it is right here, right now. Others can sense a good thing coming when it is days, months, or miles away.
>
> **MAYA ANGELOU**

I'M SURE YOU'VE HEARD of Pandora's box. If you're a curious person like me, you may sympathize with her. Imagine being given a box (more likely a jar) from Zeus himself as a gift but told you can never open it! Curiosity, understandably, gets the better of you, and you unintentionally unleash the seven deadliest sins into the world. Pandora also happened to be the first human woman created by the gods. Fascinating how many creation stories have women unleash hell on Earth: Pandora, meet Eve.

The story of Pandora's box was told in "Works and Days," written by the Greek poet Hesiod around 700 BCE, and the warning not to open Pandora's box still abounds today. Although most people have heard the tale of Pandora, few may recall what was left behind in said death jar: hope.

I've always loved this gem of a detail! Amid the awfulness and terrible fates being released upon Earth, hope remained.

Now, some scholars argue that the hope remaining in Pandora's box wasn't a blessing but a final curse. Renowned philosopher Arthur Schopenhauer wrote, "Hope is offering the illusion of comfort while keeping us in perpetual longing, and when our dreams shatter, plunging us into despair."[1] Friedrich Nietzsche took that a step further by writing, "Hope in reality is the worst of all evils, because it prolongs the torments of man."[2] Those are some dark takes on hope.

Pandora closed the lid on hope, trapping it inside before it could escape with the other deadly sins. Others interpret this act as hope remaining with the humans. All the evils spread throughout the world before returning to Olympus, yet hope remained. The elegiac poet Theognis wrote, "Hope is the only good god remaining among mankind; the others have left and gone to Olympus."[3] Perhaps hope stayed with humans as a universal promise. While humans can't control the fates, maybe we can hold tight to hope.

Centuries later, our literature still reflects the interconnectedness of hope and suffering, as evident in the novels of J. R. R. Tolkien: "The world is indeed full of peril, and in it there are many dark places; but still there is much that is fair, and though in all lands love is now mingled with grief, it grows perhaps the greater."[4] The popularity of his themes of hope demonstrates how many of us are seeking to understand how hope can exist even through hardship. Thich Nhat Hanh, the legendary Buddhist monk and peace advocate, wrote, "Hope is important because it can make the present moment less difficult to bear. If we believe that tomorrow will be better, we can bear a hardship today."[5]

I think Mark Manson summed up this duality accurately in the title of his 2019 bestselling book *Everything Is F*cked: A Book About Hope*. That said, Manson's argument—that living without hope is a better approach, so that rather than "hoping to be better" we can "be better"[6]—is actually quite a hopefilled idea, despite being packaged as the opposite!

Maybe Pandora really did trap hope for humans on Earth, or perhaps hope exists embedded within the human condition as an antidote to the inevitable suffering present in our experience. While this might not read like a hopeful start to this book, the surest thing I know about hope is that no matter what awful thing life throws at people, somehow it remains. In my work studying and teaching human resiliency and well-being for over two decades formally, and a lifetime informally, hope is the steadfast through line.

And regardless of how it got here, what truly matters is that hope *is* here. When we try to come to terms with all the pain, ill-being, and relentless challenges of our world, it's helpful to remember that no matter how much despair is present, there's always more hope waiting to be discovered.

Robyne Thinking and Driving

Driving through the outskirts of Atlanta to a basketball tournament two summers ago, with my son Jaxson asleep in the passenger seat, I heard something on a podcast that hit me like a lightning bolt: "2030 is going to be the best year. The world is going to right itself again, and we'll have decades of peace!"

I don't know about you, but I hadn't heard many people predict a bright future for humanity. Although I'm someone who deeply trusts that better days are ahead, I noticed a strong reaction in the moment to that statement. I wanted to dismiss it at first—"clearly this person hasn't watched the news lately"—but I also wanted to hear them out.

Unfortunately, the speaker's positioning wasn't overly sound. Their claims were laced with toxic positivity, essentially prosperity preaching with a side of manifestation. Now, I'm all for the power of a positive outlook, but what stood out to me most was how desperately I wanted to believe that there was hope that things were going to get better for our world. I noticed that this promise of a better tomorrow, even without evidence, brought a once-silent but nevertheless intrusive narrative to the forefront of my mind. Did I believe the world could recover? In that moment, I recognized that I was holding a spreading sense of despair for the well-being of the world. When I thought of the mess of the world we're passing on, I acknowledged to myself that I felt pretty hopeless about what the future held for my three children and their children. With nothing but open road ahead of me, I took that moment to lean into my current beliefs about the state of civilization. Who knew questioning the possibilities of human extinction was on the agenda for me that day as I kept a lookout for gas and Chick-fil-A!

This is what I asked myself:

"What do I believe to be true, in this moment, about the fate of our world?"

I invite you to answer this for yourself.

To go anywhere or to explore anything you need a starting point. What's yours? What are your current thoughts toward the future? As my dear friend Peter Katz, the brilliant singer-songwriter, encourages, notice the first answer but see if there are more answers behind those answers.

Here's what I recall thinking. My confidence in democracies had shattered as a result of knowing too many politicians and the electoral system, as well as witnessing the effects of war on both civilians and members of the military. My trust in the school system was shaky because I saw the burnout among educators who were forced to work with their hands tied and a generation of very lost and hurting kids. The three R's—reduce, reuse, recycle—didn't seem to be addressing the climate crisis. The economy was as steady as a runaway train that even Denzel Washington and Chris Pine couldn't rein in. Mental health challenges were rampant. We had more access to healthcare information, yet people were sicker than ever. Clearly AI developers hadn't seen *Terminator* or any other movie about artificial intelligence—it never ends well for the humans. My trust in the healthcare system ended in 2012 when the medical community couldn't tell me how my healthy and very much alive mother died in their care. "We have more questions than answers," they said.

Mark Manson's bestselling book about hope argues that our lives are completely meaningless and irrelevant in the big picture. TikTok is a news source. Stoicism is back in fashion after centuries. People are more connected than ever before, yet loneliness is killing more people each year than bad diets. Many of us get more love and support from strangers on the internet than from our own friends and family. And lastly, the richest and most well-resourced countries in the world are ridden with skyrocketing rates of despair, yet hope is on the rise for developing countries surviving on almost nothing—which is amazing news but also screams that something is very wrong with how Westerners are trying to live their lives. Oh, and living the "American dream" is destroying families.

As I held space for my own fears and deeply questioned where I stood on the prognosis for our world, I couldn't attribute our worldly demise to just one variable. Would it be a world war fueled by greed or the unbridled hatred toward another group for being different? Could it be from a religious movement or holy war? Or perhaps the climate crisis would wipe us out? One thing or another is likely going to radically shift our way of life. It feels inevitable. Unlike the dinosaurs' extinction, I couldn't pin our extinction or downfall to one place on the map, like the Yucatán Peninsula in Mexico. Scientists discovered the exact spot where the asteroid hit Earth, which started a chain of events that ultimately ended the dinosaurs. There'd likely be too many spots that contributed to our extinction for scientists to mark. Pandora, really, couldn't you have kept a lid on it?

I don't mean to trivialize suffering. Humor is part of resiliency—I wrote a book on that too. There's just so much wrong with almost every facet of life right now, yet we persist. We keep showing up. We're still very much here.

So, this is what I landed on to sum up my road reflection on the extinction of life as we know it. Imagine that classic R.E.M. song, the one about the end of the world and being okay with it—yes, that one, playing on a mental loop! Despite it all, I felt okay. I still held a deep sense of sadness and concern for the pain and suffering that's real and omnipresent for so many people. Yet I no longer bore the weight of the despair I'd felt earlier with the uncomfortable truths and realities of our collective fate swirling around in my mind. Why not? Because I have an inexplicable sense of confidence, faith, and hope in *people*. My work brings me into conversations and communities that capture the power of hope every day. I trust in people's abilities to change. I believe in the power of resiliency. I'm in awe of the human spirit. I see healing. I know recovery. I've even witnessed beautiful deaths.

Albert Camus explained it best: "In the midst of winter, I found there was, within me, an invincible summer."[7]

And I desperately want you to be able to find and hold your invincible summer too. I believe my life's purpose is to help people handle the hard parts of their life better, and I'm already cheering for you. Someone once asked me how I can say that I'm rooting for people I haven't even met. Well, I see people hate those they've never met all the time. I believe in the power of equal opposites, which means if it's possible to hate strangers, we can also love people we've never met. That's how I can say with full confidence I'm in your corner. Hope can be your strategy too.

In both my personal and professional lives, I've been given a gift. Not unlike Pandora's death jar, I'm able to hold hope. Despite the realities of our world at large and my own world within, which happens to have an abundance of goodness beyond measure while also being peppered with pain, loss, addictions, divorces, family dysfunction, mental health conditions, illnesses, and a full compilation of regrets, setbacks, and mistakes, I can still hold a steadfast hope in people and for people, including myself. And I want to share with you what I know, and what other people who happen to know even more than I do on this topic know about hope. Why? So you can face the realities and injustices of our unwell world, not to be paralyzed into inaction, or worse, indifference, but rather to be pulled and held together by the mightiest human thread.

I basically owe my life to hope. The very least I can do is write a book about it.

A Hopefilled Moment

Let's get carried away for a minute, get ahead of ourselves, and get our hopes up!

It's remarkable to think that something so exciting could have a negative connotation. "Don't get carried away," "Don't get ahead of yourself," "Don't get your hopes up"—people hold us back not because they're intentionally being mean, but rather as a means of protecting us. I invite you do just this and see how it feels!

What are the biggest hopes you hold for yourself right now? How about the biggest hopes you hold for others?

Just for a moment, imagine that these hopes have all come to pass. Sit in the presence of all your hopes unfolding in perfect timing.

Notice what it feels like. Are the edges of your mouth pointing upward to the heavens? Do you feel the natural draw to lift your arms up to the sky in triumph? Or the urge to pump your fist in victory? Has the tension in your body shifted to a sense of ease?

Who in your life would be most impacted by these hopes coming true? How does that make you feel? Look at your loved ones' faces and feel their energy as they experience the moment of realization that what they've hoped for is upon them.

Imagine the conversation where you're sharing your realized hopes with someone who matters to you. What words are exchanged? What emotions are present?

Whether what you hope for unfolds exactly as you envision or takes shape in ways beyond your wildest dreams, notice the profound impact that evoking hope has on both your body and mind. Our thoughts have the power to transform our emotional landscape. By allowing yourself to escape into a realm of hopefilled imagination, you create a sanctuary—a place for refuge, inspiration, and even just a brief, restorative pause. If we so readily envision the worst-case scenarios, then it's only fair to grant ourselves equal time to imagine the best ones too. Call it daydreaming, wishful thinking, or positive mental gymnastics—the results are the same. We can use hope to catch a feeling of bliss in our very own mental playground.

Why This Works

Allowing yourself to get carried away, get ahead of yourself, and get your hopes up taps into the power of positive visualization, which has been shown to enhance motivation and well-being. From a psychological perspective, this exercise leverages the broaden-and-build theory, coined by Barbara Fredrickson, which suggests that positive emotions expand our awareness and encourage novel, varied, and exploratory thoughts and actions. By permitting ourselves to hope and imagine positive outcomes, we not only foster optimism, but also increase our resiliency (by seeing a way through) and our creativity (for imagining what it would take to get there). This practice ultimately reduces anxiety by shifting focus from fear of disappointment to possibility and potential, creating a safe space for emotional exploration, curiosity, and growth. You are one hope-filled thought away from feeling better.

2
Hopscotching Through Hope's History

> # History is a vast early warning system.
>
> **NORMAN COUSINS**

Have you ever been working on a task that needs to get done, but in the process of trying to get it done, you go down the proverbial rabbit hole? Dear reader, consider this the "history of hope" rabbit hole!

The concept of hope has captivated minds and hearts across cultures and eras. From ancient sages to modern thinkers, countless individuals have explored the essence of hope—what it means, how it shapes our decisions, and why it's essential for our well-being and society. Imagine hope as a dazzling thread that shimmers brightly in the fabric of history, connecting us from ancient civilizations to contemporary movements. It's not just a concept; it's a living, breathing force that has inspired individuals and even sparked revolutions, from the ancient streets of Athens to the social media reels of today.

Jumping into the chronology of hope reminds me of the first ever "Ted Talk" I saw growing up. It was *Bill & Ted's Excellent Adventure* (and it was most excellent). In the movie, two students traveled through time to bring history alive for their final project. Now you and I can hopscotch through history together to learn about some theories and hope movements that have radically impacted our understanding and practices of hope as we now know it.

First Stop: Greece

Let's start our journey in ancient Greece, where philosophers like Aristotle and the Stoics were the original hope enthusiasts. Aristotle, the ultimate life coach of fourth century BCE, introduced us to "eudaimonia," or the good life. He believed that hope wasn't just wishful thinking; it was a motivating force that propelled us toward virtuous actions. Picture Aristotle pacing under the olive trees, encouraging his students to embrace hope as they navigated the complexities of life. For him, hope wasn't merely a passive state; it was active engagement with the world, urging individuals to pursue their highest potential.

Fast-forward a century, and the Stoics entered the scene with their rational take on hope. Think of Seneca and Epictetus as your calm, collected friends who helped you maintain perspective in challenging times. They taught that hope was an expectation aligned with virtue, a sturdy lifeboat amid life's unpredictable storms. Imagine these philosophers calmly contemplating the power of hope to keep spirits buoyant even when the seas of existence grew choppy. Their teachings emphasized resiliency and the importance of maintaining a hopeful disposition, encouraging individuals to cultivate inner strength and optimism.

Over to Thirteenth-Century Italy

Now, let's jump ahead to the medieval era, where the brilliant Saint Thomas Aquinas stepped into the spotlight. He took hope to a whole new level, defining it as a theological virtue that emphasized trust in God's promises. Aquinas made hope a daily companion for moral decision-making, adding the power of the divine to our understanding. Imagine medieval scholars in candlelit rooms, deeply engrossed in discussions about how hope could guide them through moral dilemmas and shape their communities. Aquinas's vision of hope invited individuals to look beyond their immediate struggles and trust in a greater good, reinforcing the idea that hope is intertwined with faith.

Next Stop: Renaissance and Enlightenment

Then comes the Renaissance and Enlightenment—oh, what a vibrant explosion of ideas! Think of this as the grand party where hope donned new attire. Thinkers like Blaise Pascal and Immanuel Kant celebrated human agency, showcasing hope as essential in our quest for meaning. Pascal's insights highlighted the tension between faith and reason, while Kant encouraged individuals to act according to principles that could be universally applied. Friedrich Nietzsche, on the other hand, threw in a bit of mischief, challenging traditional notions of hope and urging individuals to craft their own destinies in a seemingly godless world. Imagine the divisiveness of these lively debates, where philosophers argued passionately over who got to define hope, questioned whether there was a God, and introduced the believe-just-in-case approach! Adding to this rich tapestry, Mary Wollstonecraft later built on these ideas, advocating for women's rights and education in her seminal work *A Vindication of the Rights of Woman*.[1] Her vision inspired hope for a future of gender equality, reinforcing the notion that hope fuels social change and empowerment.

Hope Across the Pond

But hold on—hope didn't stop evolving there! Meet Ralph Waldo Emerson, the American essayist who could be considered the original life coach of the nineteenth century, or even the first blogger. He published his thoughts on random topics to share with audiences he never even met! Emerson emphasized self-reliance and societal growth, advocating for a hopeful outlook as a catalyst for both individual and community empowerment. His essays encouraged individuals to trust their intuition and embrace the boundless possibilities of life. Picture a gathering of inspired souls discussing how hope can fuel innovation and progress, surrounded by the beauty of nature, as they passionately explore the connections between hope, creativity, and the human spirit.

Psychology Joins In

As we roll into the twentieth century, psychology takes on a leading role, with hope seen as a cornerstone of resiliency and psychological well-being. Dr. Viktor Frankl emerges from adversity, illuminating the essential role hope plays in overcoming life's challenges. His insights remind us that even in the darkest of times, hope can be a beacon. Frankl's experience as a Holocaust survivor shaped his understanding that the pursuit of meaning, grounded in hope, is vital for survival.[2] Meanwhile, Dr. Albert Bandura introduces the concept of self-efficacy—our belief in our capabilities that enhances our hopeful outlook. Imagine a room full of psychologists exchanging ideas, like a brainstorming session with the goal of making a playbook for how to live hopefilled in every and any season of your life.

Dr. Charles R. Snyder coins hope theory, which argues that there are three main components that make up hopeful thinking. These magic ingredients are goals (approaching life in a goal-oriented way), pathways (finding different ways to achieve our goals), and agency (believing that we can instigate change and achieve these goals).[3] His research shows that hope isn't just an individual pursuit: It thrives in communities, fostering solidarity and collective action. Dr. Snyder's work illustrates that hope can be nurtured through setting realistic goals, developing pathways to achieve them, and fostering the belief that one can succeed. Picture communities coming together, hearts and minds united in the pursuit of a shared dream, creating ripples of hope that spread far and wide.

And then we have narrative identity theory, introduced by Dr. Dan P. McAdams. This concept highlights how personal stories shape our understanding of hope, which can be powerful for trauma survivors. Imagine a circle of individuals sharing their journeys, transforming pain into purpose, and cultivating hope and resiliency through the power of storytelling. It's a beautiful reminder that our experiences, when shared, can illuminate paths for others.

We've covered a lot of ground here, and of course, there are millions of other stops and key thinkers who have contributed to our perspectives of hope as we know it to be today. To see these historical perspectives in action, let's travel back in time once more for a brief look at how hope played out across historical movements. Why? Because historical events fueled with hope have radically shaped the world as we know it today and what's possible for our tomorrows.

Hope Across Historical Movements

Hope has been a powerful catalyst for social change. Each movement is a testament to the belief that a brighter future is possible—a faith deeply rooted in the human experience.

Let's rewind to ancient Mesopotamia, where the Code of Hammurabi was crafted around 1754 BCE. This ancient legal framework was built on the hope for justice and social order, setting a precedent for societies to aspire to fairness. Picture ancient scribes diligently carving laws into stone, driven by the hope of creating a harmonious society. The Code, with its emphasis on accountability and fairness, illustrates how the aspiration for justice has been foundational to human civilization.

In ancient Egypt, the concept of "Ma'at" embodied truth, balance, and order. Egyptians believed that maintaining Ma'at was vital for societal harmony. Imagine priests and philosophers collaborating to ensure that order prevailed, driven by the hope that their efforts would create a better world—one that would endure even beyond their lifetimes. The pursuit of Ma'at was not only a religious duty but a hopeful vision for a prosperous society where justice and order reigned supreme.

As we leap into the Age of Revolutions, hope takes center stage once more. The American Revolution (1775-1783) was an uprising fueled by the hope for self-governance. Thomas Jefferson's Declaration of Independence proclaimed that all men were created equal, igniting a fire of hope that inspired colonists to rise against British rule. Picture passionate debates in candlelit taverns as revolutionaries exchanged ideas about liberty and justice. The revolution was fueled by the belief that a new nation could be built on the principles of equality and democracy, forever altering the course of history.

Not far behind was the French Revolution (1789-1799), where the rallying cry of "Liberté, égalité, fraternité!" united the masses in their pursuit of equality and justice. Imagine the streets filled with fervent revolutionaries, hopeful for a future where oppression was dismantled and democracy reigned supreme! The revolutionaries believed that through collective action and hope, they could create a society free from tyranny, a belief that resonated across Europe and inspired future movements for change.

Fast-forward to the nineteenth century, where hope fueled the abolitionist movements. Figures like Frederick Douglass in the United States and William Wilberforce in Britain were champions of justice, motivated by the hope for freedom and human dignity. Douglass's powerful assertion "If there is no struggle, there is no progress"[4] captures the essence of how hope intertwines with action to bring about meaningful change. These leaders rallied their communities, using hope as a tool to challenge the status quo and advocate for the rights of the oppressed.

In Canada, hope has also played a pivotal role in movements for justice, particularly regarding Indigenous rights. The Truth and Reconciliation Commission of Canada (TRC), established in 2008, sought to address the legacy of residential schools and foster healing between Indigenous and non-Indigenous communities. The TRC's calls to action are rooted in a hope for reconciliation, emphasizing that acknowledging past injustices can pave the way for a more equitable future. This movement underscores the belief that hope can guide us toward understanding, healing, and rebuilding trust.

The Canadian women's suffrage movement is another poignant example. Leaders like Nellie McClung and Emily Murphy fought tirelessly for women's rights, fueled by the hope that women could achieve equality in a patriarchal society. McClung's passionate declaration that women are going to form a chain, a greater sisterhood than the world has ever known, underscores the hope that enfranchisement would empower women to effect societal change.[5] The suffragists united under a shared vision of equality, inspiring future generations to continue the fight for women's rights.

As we journey into the twentieth century, hope emerges as a central theme in various global movements for justice. The civil rights movement in the United States, led by figures like Dr. Martin Luther King Jr., showcased hope's role in the fight against racial injustice. Dr. King's iconic "I Have a Dream" speech painted a vision of a racially integrated society, emphasizing that hope could transcend deep-seated racism.[6] His belief that "the arc of the moral universe is long, but it bends toward justice" highlights hope as an active pursuit of equity.[7] King's message of love, unity, and hope resonates to this day, inspiring countless movements around the globe.

The anti-apartheid movement in South Africa is another shining example of hope's transformative power. Nelson Mandela and Desmond Tutu galvanized the nation with their vision of reconciliation and equality. Mandela's assertion "It always seems impossible until it is done" embodies the spirit of hope driving the struggle against apartheid.[8] Picture vibrant rallies and passionate speeches, with hope as the fuel propelling individuals to challenge an oppressive regime. Their collective hope inspired a nation to rise, transforming despair into resiliency.

Now, let's soar into the mid-twentieth century, when the space race captured the imagination of humanity. The launch of Sputnik-1 by the Soviet Union in 1957 ignited a spark of hope and ambition in the United States, leading to the Apollo program and the historic moon landing in 1969. US President John F. Kennedy's famous words "We choose to go to the moon not because it is easy, but because it is hard" encapsulated the spirit of hope that characterized this era.[9] The space race represented humanity's hope for exploration, progress, and unity beyond our planet, fueling technological advancements and igniting dreams of what could be achieved when we dared to reach for the stars.

In contemporary times, hope continues to fuel movements for social justice, environmental sustainability, and human rights. The #MeToo movement, which gained momentum in 2017, exemplifies hope for a world free from sexual harassment and violence. Founded by activist Tarana Burke and later popularized by celebrities speaking out, the movement has empowered countless individuals to share their stories, fostering a collective hope for accountability and societal change. The phrase "Believe women" embodies the hope for justice and support for survivors, sparking discussions around consent and respect.

The global youth climate strikes, inspired by Greta Thunberg, represent a hopeful uprising of young people advocating for urgent action against climate change. Events like Fridays for Future mobilize millions of students worldwide, reflecting the hope that their voices will lead to meaningful policy changes. The determination of these young activists demonstrates that hope can drive a generation to demand a sustainable future, reinforcing the belief that collective action can effect significant change.

That was a lot!

I appreciate that was quite the rabbit hole, and it does serve a purpose. As we stand at the intersection of history and hope, let's remember that hope is more than just a feel-good topic or a warm and fuzzy idea. It's a powerful catalyst for change. It transcends time, culture, and circumstance, inviting us to envision a brighter future. Whether it's in the ancient streets of Athens, the revolutionary fervor of France, or our modern movements for justice and equality, hope remains a vibrant thread connecting us to each other and to our best selves.

While this is by no means an exhaustive account of all things "hope" since the dawn of time, this snapshot shows that hope has always been an effective vehicle for understanding and meeting obstacles at one time deemed unexplainable, insurmountable, or impossible. Hope is so much more than wishful thinking for dreamers or a useless practice for us naive Pollyannas. It's a time-tested strategy woven through the fabric of all humankind.

Your Personal Hope Timeline

Let's play with our very own power of hope by mapping our own experiences of hopeful thinking and action over time, just like the changemakers and thinkers explored in this chapter.

Instructions

1. **Draw your hope timeline.** On a blank page or in your journal, draw a horizontal timeline starting from your earliest memories to today.

2. **Identify five to seven key "hope moments."** Reflect on moments in your life when hope played a role, whether quietly as a belief things could get better or boldly as a catalyst for action. These could be times of challenge when you held on to hope, moments when you chose to believe in a better outcome despite uncertainty, situations where hope helped you motivate others, or events that inspired you toward justice, learning, or connection.

3. **Label each moment.** For each moment, jot down the following:

- the year or your age
- a short title (e.g., "The Year I Didn't Give Up")
- a sentence or two about what hope looked like for you in that moment

By creating your personal hope timeline and identifying the moments when hope moved you forward, you join a long lineage of thinkers, changemakers, and quiet revolutionaries who have used hope as a guide. Just like the ancient philosophers and modern visionaries we met in this chapter, your story adds to the rich and ongoing history of hope in action.

Can you look beyond the challenges, setbacks, and stressors of today, and see the elements of your life that you once hoped for? How many times has life surprised you for the better? Sometimes, recognizing the hopes we've already realized is the clearest reminder that hope is not only historical, but also deeply personal and still very much alive.

Why This Works

This exercise brings your personal journey with hope into sharp focus. By reflecting on past moments where hope guided your thoughts and actions, you're actively practicing the art of self-awareness—a key component in cultivating emotional resiliency. Mapping your hope timeline allows you to see patterns, track growth, and recognize the role hope has played in getting you through life's toughest moments. This not only reinforces the idea that hope is a force that propels us forward, but also strengthens your belief in your capacity to navigate the future with hope as your compass.

In addition, this exercise taps into the psychology of narrative-building. Research shows that when we actively narrate our lives, especially with a focus on positive themes, we enhance our sense of purpose and agency. You begin to view your story as one of resilience, not just survival, allowing hope to become a more tangible, actionable presence in your life. It's a way of charting the course for future goals by recognizing the moments where hope truly made a difference. As you reflect on your journey, you'll likely find that hope wasn't just a fleeting thought—it was the invisible thread weaving through your successes, guiding you toward better outcomes and more meaningful connections. The practice of looking back with purpose helps you unlock the strength to move forward with even more conviction, knowing that hope isn't just a fleeting concept—it's a lived experience, one that's shaped who you are and who you continue to become.

3

The Costs of Hopelessness and the Need for a Samwise Gamgee

> What is it that needs doing,
> that I know something about,
> that probably won't happen
> unless I take responsibility for it?

BUCKMINSTER FULLER

IMAGINE THAT you're sixteen years old and everyone is talking about their future. You're a junior in high school and teachers, parents, and even random strangers ask you about your plans after high school. You hear your peers talking about schools, trades, or travel, while grown-ups either reminisce about their senior years of high school being the glory days or tell you how they couldn't wait to graduate and get on with their lives.

You, on the other hand. You try to look into your future and all you see is absolute nothingness. You try to imagine even what next month could look like, and you aren't there. You can picture your family in the future, but you're missing. You can visualize your peers heading off into their bright futures, but you can't see yourself anywhere. Because you don't exist in any tomorrow.

I once described my depression as my body's inability to hold hope.

I believe that each person has a tiny and tender pilot light in their soul that keeps the will to live alive. Once the flame is extinguished, your future disappears with it. That is what happened to me at sixteen years old. My light going out didn't happen with one sudden gust; it was a slow, untraceable current that smothered me while I was in the process of screaming for help. I also believe that the people who need the most help ask for it in all the wrong ways. Fighting a force beyond the scope of what any child could articulate, I asked for help in the form of addiction, self-harm, self-sabotage, and burning relationship bridges at every turn. In hindsight, I wished I could have explained to those who loved me the most that I was fighting intrusive thoughts, violent impulses, and emotional agony. I didn't at the time because despite how scared I was, the thought of my mother also having to carry my burden gutted me. I wanted to protect her at all costs, regardless of the price I had to pay. Some may call this feeling despair, the opposite of hope. To me, despair doesn't capture it because you can feel despair. I felt nothing, complete and total numbness. In those moments, what I needed most wasn't a solution—I needed a Samwise Gamgee. Someone steady and loyal, who could sit beside me in the darkness, not trying to fix it, but reminding me that I wasn't alone. Samwise didn't carry the One Ring, but he carried Frodo when Frodo could no longer carry himself. That's the kind of hope I needed—one that shows up, even when things seem unbearable.

Hopelessness is a profound emotional state that reaches far beyond temporary sadness or disappointment. It's the loss of belief that things can improve, that our actions matter, or that life holds meaning. Hopelessness is not only an internal battle—it impacts how we live, work, and interact with the world. From individuals battling personal challenges to companies grappling with disengaged workforces or stagnant products, and societies facing economic and social breakdowns, the cost of hopelessness is staggering. In this chapter, we'll explore how hopelessness manifests on three levels: individual, organizational, and societal.

The Cost of Hopelessness to Individuals and Families

For an individual, hopelessness is like being trapped in a room without doors or windows. Every attempt to improve feels futile, and this deep sense of helplessness can permeate every aspect of life. Hopelessness affects emotional health, physical well-being, behavior, and even financial stability. Research shows that hopelessness is closely linked to mental health issues such as depression, anxiety, and suicidal ideation. According to researchers, hopelessness is one of the strongest predictors of suicidal thoughts, as individuals who feel that their situation is unchangeable are more likely to contemplate or die by suicide.[1] Beyond mental health, hopelessness also impacts physical well-being. Studies indicate that individuals experiencing chronic hopelessness often exhibit elevated stress hormones like cortisol, which can weaken the immune system, increase the risk of cardiovascular disease, and lead to sleep disturbances.[2]

The impact of hopelessness on physical health can also extend to chronic conditions. For example, research shows that individuals with chronic illnesses, such as diabetes or heart disease, who experience hopelessness tend to have worse health outcomes.[3] Hopelessness can hinder their motivation to adhere to treatment plans or seek medical care, exacerbating their condition.

Behaviorally, hopeless individuals may disengage from work, relationships, and self-care, leading to isolation, a decline in productivity, and a reduced quality of life. The National Institute of Mental Health notes that individuals struggling with hopelessness are less likely to seek out opportunities for growth or improvement, reinforcing a cycle of stagnation and despair.[4] In essence, hopelessness doesn't just affect how people feel; it affects how they live, contributing to emotional, physical, and financial struggles that compound over time.

An individual's hopelessness can have profound effects on their families as well. Studies show that family members, especially children, are particularly vulnerable to the emotional and behavioral consequences of a loved one's hopelessness. Research published in the *Journal of Family Psychology* highlights how parental hopelessness can lead to deteriorating relationships, increased stress within the family unit, and a breakdown in emotional support structures.[5] Children in such environments often experience higher levels of anxiety and depression as they absorb the emotional state of their parents. Furthermore, hopelessness within a family can disrupt communication, lead to emotional withdrawal, and increase the likelihood of children inheriting mental health challenges. In essence, when one member of a family feels hopeless, the entire family system can suffer, perpetuating cycles of despair that may affect multiple generations.

In addition to the emotional toll, hopelessness can also have financial consequences for families. A study from Rutgers found that households dealing with hopelessness are more likely to experience economic instability.[6] This may manifest in higher rates of unemployment, difficulty managing household finances, or increased reliance on social services. Financial stress, in turn, exacerbates feelings of despair, creating a feedback loop where economic challenges fuel emotional hopelessness, and vice versa.

Another example comes from families caring for loved ones with chronic illnesses. According to the National Alliance for Caregiving, caregivers who feel emotionally drained and hopeless about a loved one's prognosis often experience burnout, characterized by emotional exhaustion, anxiety, and hopelessness.[7] This hopelessness can strain family relationships and leave caregivers feeling isolated and unsupported. Over time, this emotional burden impacts all family members, reducing their ability to offer care and support while perpetuating cycles of stress and hopelessness.

The Cost of Hopelessness to Organizations

Hopelessness does not remain confined to the private sphere. It can spread across entire organizations, eroding workplace morale, reducing productivity, and driving away talent. When employees lose hope, either in their own potential or in the company's future, the entire organization suffers.

Research shows that only about 31 percent of employees in the United States and Canada are engaged at work, with many citing burnout, lack of recognition, or stagnant career progression as reasons for their disengagement.[8] When employees lose hope in their ability to succeed within an organization, they disengage. This can lead to presenteeism, where workers are physically present but mentally checked out, and ultimately to burnout.

Since the onset of COVID-19, burnout rates have soared. In the United States, nearly half of healthcare professionals reported burnout during the pandemic,[9] and 52 percent of employees overall reported becoming burned out within the past year.[10] In Canada, 24 to 69 percent of workers report burnout or related symptoms, with frontline healthcare staff among the hardest hit.[11] Internationally, McKinsey found that approximately one in four employees experienced burnout—underscoring its global scope.[12]

The pandemic has blurred the boundaries between work and personal life, compounded by long hours, increased workloads, and persistent stress. These rising burnout rates not only impact individual well-being but also create ripple effects throughout organizations, leading to decreased productivity, higher absenteeism, and increased turnover as employees struggle to manage the demands of the post-pandemic workplace. Burnout can often lead to feelings of hopelessness, as prolonged stress, exhaustion, and a sense of overwhelm erode an individual's belief that their efforts can lead to meaningful change, trapping them in a cycle of despair and disengagement.

Hopelessness in the workplace creates a ripple effect. Disengaged employees are less creative, less productive, and more likely to leave. Turnover becomes costly, and the loss of institutional knowledge further weakens the organization. As reported by Payactiv, replacing an employee can cost anywhere from 50 to 200 percent of their annual salary, depending on their position.[13] Hopelessness directly impacts a company's bottom line. And the inverse is also true: Gallup found that companies with engaged employees are 23 percent more profitable and 18 percent more productive.[14] When employees stop believing in the future of the organization or their role within it, innovation halts. No one pushes for new ideas or takes creative risks because they no longer see the point. Additionally, when hopelessness becomes part of the company culture, it affects recruitment. Talented employees won't join a company where the environment feels toxic or stagnant. The company's reputation suffers, making it harder to attract and retain top talent. In contrast, organizations that foster hope by connecting employees to a larger mission and providing opportunities for growth see higher levels of engagement, creativity, and overall performance.

The Cost of Hopelessness to Society

At a societal level, hopelessness has far-reaching consequences that can affect both economic and social well-being.

When entire communities or nations lose hope, it creates ripple effects that can lead to stagnation in key areas such as workforce participation, productivity, and economic growth. World Bank studies show that countries facing high levels of societal disengagement often experience slower economic development and rising poverty rates.[15] When individuals lose hope in their ability to improve their circumstances, they may disengage from meaningful participation in the economy, leading to underemployment and reduced consumer spending.

Moreover, hopelessness can deepen economic inequality. As mentioned earlier, individuals who feel trapped by their circumstances may lack the motivation or resources to pursue education or new opportunities, which can widen the gap between different socioeconomic groups. This lack of upward mobility not only affects individuals but also hinders societal progress, creating systemic cycles of poverty that are difficult to escape and holding back entire communities' economic growth.

However, the dynamics of hopelessness differ across the world. In many developed countries, hope is waning as people face increasing concerns over job insecurity, wage stagnation, political polarization, and growing inequality. Citizens may feel that the systems meant to support them—education, healthcare, and government—

are failing, which fuels a sense of being stuck, helpless, and powerless. In contrast, many developing countries are seeing the opposite trend: Hope is rising as new opportunities emerge. Rapid economic growth, improved access to education, and expanding technology are creating a sense of optimism, with many people seeing a clearer path to a better future.[16] This contrast shows that societal hope is closely tied to the perception of opportunity and progress. Where individuals see potential for improvement, hope thrives, but where opportunities seem to be shrinking, hopelessness takes root.

The political costs of hopelessness, too, are staggering. Communities facing hopelessness often experience reduced social cohesion and lower levels of civic engagement. In a recorded conversation shared by the Harvard Kennedy School, political scientist Robert Putnam emphasizes the role of social capital—networks of relationships and trust—in maintaining strong, connected communities. When social capital erodes, communities can become fragmented, and people may feel more isolated and disconnected from one another.[17]

This disengagement can manifest in lower voter turnout, less participation in community activities, and a decrease in volunteerism. When individuals feel their voices don't matter, the decline of civic engagement can lead to heightened social tensions and, in extreme cases, unrest or violence. Hopelessness can also foster mistrust in essential social systems, such as courts, schools, and government, as people become disillusioned with the institutions that are supposed to serve and protect them.

Lastly, hopelessness has dire consequences for technological innovation. A recent example from the United States is the fluctuation in start-up activity during the COVID-19 pandemic. While the country saw an initial drop in new business formations in early 2020 due to economic uncertainty and anxiety, this trend quickly reversed. According to the US Census Bureau's Business Formation Statistics, after a sharp decline in March and April, new business applications surged to record highs later in the year, particularly in sectors like e-commerce.[18] This shift illustrates how initial hopelessness can hinder innovation, but renewed optimism can stimulate technological progress. In societies where hopelessness is pervasive, the drive for innovation may also fade. When people stop believing that change is possible, they're less likely to push for improvements, making it harder to tackle the very problems that contributed to the hopelessness in the first place.

Hopelessness is not a passive state—it's an active force of erosion. It quietly strips away potential, disconnects individuals from their futures, and paralyzes organizations and societies. It's a thief that robs us of our capacity to imagine change, to believe that tomorrow can be better. If left unchecked, hopelessness creates a void where growth, connection, and progress should reside. But here's the thing: We've been here before. This fight is winnable, but it requires a united effort.

It may feel overwhelming, but the alternative is unthinkable. As Rocky Balboa says often in the famous movie series, his approach to life's challenges isn't about how hard you get hit, it's about how hard you get hit and keep moving forward. The reality is that the battle against hopelessness isn't about avoiding pain or adversity—it's about refusing to let that pain define us. It's about getting back up, time and time again, and pushing forward. We don't have the luxury of waiting for someone else to fix this; it starts with us, right now, making the choice to lean into hope. And I'm glad to be here to show you how to do exactly that.

Hope doesn't always come in grand gestures. Sometimes, it looks like quiet loyalty. Like someone refusing to give up on you. Like Samwise, who reminded Frodo—and all of us—that even when you can't see the light, you can borrow someone else's until you remember your own. That's the kind of presence that helps extinguish hopelessness—not with platitudes, but with persistence. So, let's get to work. Let's decide to not just face hopelessness but actively fight it—within ourselves, within our organizations, and within society. Because as Samwise, Frodo's loyal friend, unlikely spiritual guide, and the real hero in the classic series, reminded us during the darkest moments, "There's some good in this world, Mr. Frodo, and it's worth fighting for."[19] And that good begins with hope.

Real Talk with Robyne: Confronting Personal Hopelessness

The true cost of personal hopelessness is immeasurable, not just because we can't quantify lost potential, but because we can never truly know the ripple effects of dreams that were never pursued. I invite you to engage in a courageous reflection exercise. Approach it gently, and remember: The discomfort or raw honesty that may surface holds the power for the greatest breakthroughs. This is a space for radical honesty. No excuses, no sugarcoating, no BS, no judgment. Just real talk and real thoughts.

Ask yourself:

- What is truly holding you back from leaning into the biggest hopes for your life?

- Go beyond surface-level fears. What are the deep-rooted beliefs or narratives that keep you from daring to dream big?

- When you hear that inner critic, whose voice does it echo? Is it yours, or does it sound like someone from your past—a parent, a teacher, an old boss? Who first planted the seeds of doubt that made you feel unworthy, undeserving, or selfish for wanting more?

- What is the real cost of playing it safe? Consider not just the missed opportunities but the emotional toll of unfulfilled potential. What joy, growth, or impact are you sacrificing by staying small?

- What dreams have been placed on your heart that you aren't pursuing? What would it mean for you, and for others, if you were to honor those dreams?

Why This Works

Asking hard questions isn't just about confronting discomfort; it's about unlocking growth. From a psychological perspective, this exercise taps into the power of cognitive behavioral therapy techniques, which encourage individuals to challenge and reframe negative thought patterns. By naming fears, identifying limiting beliefs, and tracing them back to their origins, you disrupt the cycle of automatic negative thinking.

Additionally, self-inquiry and introspection are key components of emotional intelligence, the ability to understand and manage your emotions. When you engage in deep reflection, you increase self-awareness, reduce cognitive dissonance, and enhance emotional resiliency. This process allows you to break free from mental constraints and align more closely with your authentic self, paving the way for greater hope, creativity, and fulfillment.

4

Key Hope Theories and a Few Good News Stories

"

Some changes look negative on the surface, but you will soon realize that space is being created in your life for something new to emerge.

ECKHART TOLLE

HOPE IS THE QUIET, unbreakable thread woven through the human experience. It's what keeps us grounded in times of peace and holds us when life feels overwhelming. Hope is so much more than a wish; it's a force that takes shape within us, guiding our thoughts, fueling our actions, and offering us purpose when things fall apart. As Dr. Viktor Frankl reminds us, "Everything can be taken from a man but one thing: the last of the human freedoms—to choose one's attitude in any given set of circumstances, to choose one's own way."[1] At the heart of hope lies this truth that regardless of our circumstances, we hold power within ourselves to shape our response and see a way forward. In the next few chapters, we'll build the blueprint to do just that.

To start, let's consider the story of the Chilean miners, trapped over 2,000 feet underground after a catastrophic collapse in 2010.[2] For sixty-nine days, these thirty-three miners endured unbearable conditions, relying on shared hope and resiliency to sustain one another until they could be rescued. They rationed food, shared prayers, and kept their spirits alive through the unshakable belief that they would make it out together. Their story reminds us that hope is both deeply personal and profoundly collective. They've shown us how hope, shared and nurtured, can light a path through even the darkest tunnels.

And sometimes, hope appears in simpler but equally powerful stories, like that of Arthur, the stray dog who joined a team of adventure racers as they crossed a treacherous jungle in Ecuador.[3] During the grueling Adventure Racing World Championship, a team of Swedish athletes shared a meatball with a scrappy stray they met along the trail. To their surprise, Arthur decided to stay with them, trudging alongside them through dense jungle, over mountains, and across rivers. Despite muddy terrain, harsh weather, and exhaustion, Arthur refused to leave the team's side, even swimming across rivers to stay with his new friends. His unwavering determination and loyalty touched the team, and by the end of the race, they couldn't imagine leaving him behind. They arranged to bring Arthur home to Sweden, where he lived with the team captain, Mikael Lindnord. Arthur's journey embodies the essence of hope: It's the steadfast commitment to something greater, even when the path is filled with obstacles.

To help us grasp the power and possibility of the hope interwoven in these powerful stories, let's review three theories that show us how hope can be a steady companion and a transformative catalyst, illuminating paths that might otherwise be hidden. Together, these hope theories create a multifaceted understanding of hope that can guide us as we reflect on our own lives and the lives of those we seek to support.

Dr. Snyder's Goal-Oriented Hope Theory

Dr. Charles R. Snyder, a leading psychologist of the late twentieth century, provided one of the most practical and widely used definitions of hope. In his view, hope isn't just a passive feeling but rather an active, cognitive state that includes a particular set of thoughts and evokes a sense of possibility, which leads to action. This mindset combines clear goals with the strategies to achieve them. Dr. Snyder's approach is both straightforward and empowering: In his view, hope is the foundation of purposeful action, encouraging us to actively pursue what we find meaningful.

At the heart of Dr. Snyder's hope theory are three interconnected components.

1 **Goals thinking:** This is where hope begins. Goals thinking represents our ability to identify and focus on goals that are personally valuable and meaningful. Whether it's a career ambition, a dream to learn a new skill, or even a hope for a better future, setting clear goals gives hope a direction. Without goals, hope has nowhere to aim: It's just a feeling without form.

2 **Pathways thinking:** Once we have a goal in mind, we need strategies to reach it. Pathways thinking is about creating multiple routes, thinking through how we will get from point A to point B. Dr. Snyder's research found that hope involves envisioning not just one path but several ways forward, each adaptable to life's unpredictable twists and turns. This kind of thinking encourages flexibility and creativity, helping us stay hopeful even when things don't go as planned.

3. **Agency thinking:** Finally, hope requires us to believe that we have the ability to initiate and sustain action toward our goals. Agency thinking is the motivation to keep going, the inner dialogue that says, *I can do this.* In Dr. Snyder's view, hope isn't just about having a goal and a plan; it's also about having the determination to pursue them, even when we encounter obstacles.

Dr. Snyder's hope theory is especially powerful in its emphasis on action. Hope isn't just a vague wish; it's a structured way of thinking that encourages us to pursue the things that matter to us. Consider the story of Michael Jordan, often hailed as one of the greatest basketball players of all time. After being cut from his high school team, Jordan could have let doubt overshadow his dreams. Instead, he maintained a clear vision of excelling in basketball (goals thinking), committed to relentless practice (pathways thinking), and believed in his ability to persevere through every setback (agency thinking). His hope became a powerful force that propelled him to become a six-time NBA champion and an icon of resiliency.

Similarly, Serena Williams faced significant challenges on her path to tennis greatness. From financial struggles to societal barriers, she was no stranger to adversity. Yet she had a vivid goal: to become the world's best in her sport (goals thinking). She built her path through rigorous training, mental discipline, and an unwavering commitment to growth (pathways thinking), believing in her capacity to succeed regardless of obstacles (agency thinking). Her hope and tenacity have made her a twenty-three-time Grand Slam champion and a beacon of inspiration worldwide.

Dr. Snyder's perspective shows us that hope, when anchored in clear goals, adaptive strategies, and unshakable self-belief, is one of the most transformative motivators we have.

Dr. Frankl's Existential Hope and Theory of Meaning

When I was institutionalized at sixteen years old, I was gifted the book *Man's Search for Meaning* by a hospital volunteer. Little did I know that this one book would radically change my life and set me on the path of studying psychology, if I could just survive high school.

Dr. Viktor Frankl, an Austrian psychiatrist and Holocaust survivor, introduced a perspective on hope from a deeply existential place. For Dr. Frankl, hope was inseparable from humanity's search for meaning, especially in the face of suffering. His 1946 book (translated into English in 1959) describes how, even in the harsh conditions of concentration camps, those who held on to a sense of purpose and meaning were more likely to survive. Hope to him meant finding light in the darkest of places, clinging to purpose when everything else felt lost.

Dr. Frankl's theory of meaning suggests that humans are driven by what he called a "will to meaning," a fundamental need to make sense of life's events and find purpose, even in suffering. Hope, then, becomes a bridge to this sense of meaning, allowing us to endure by connecting our lives to something larger than ourselves. For Dr. Frankl, hope wasn't simply about envisioning a better outcome; it was about creating meaning from experiences, even those that seem overwhelmingly bleak. It's so important for me to clarify that this isn't about seeking meaning as in "Why is this happening to me?" or "There's a silver lining in everything." Do I even believe those things? Hell, no. Some things are plain awful, cruel, and even evil. Meaning, as Dr. Frankl explained it, is about saying yes to life despite everything. He emphasized the power to choose meaning in the present moment. For Dr. Frankl, meaning was not a passive discovery but an active creation. It was about finding purpose through choices, even when faced with unavoidable suffering. He believed that meaning could be found in three ways: through work or deeds, through experiences and relationships, and through the attitude one takes toward suffering. In his view, meaning was less about answering, "Why is this happening?" and more about asking, "How can I respond to this?" This perspective allowed individuals to maintain dignity and purpose, even in the most dehumanizing circumstances. For Dr. Frankl, meaning was the ultimate expression of human freedom—the power to choose one's response, to assert one's humanity, and to affirm life, no matter the situation.

This view is especially valuable when life presents us with circumstances beyond our control. While Dr. Snyder's theory of hope encourages us to pursue achievable goals, Dr. Frankl's approach teaches us to find hope in the belief that our lives have inherent value, regardless of the outcomes we face. Consider the story of Christopher Reeve, the acclaimed actor best known for his role as Superman, who was paralyzed from the neck down after a tragic horseback riding accident. Reeve could have easily fallen into despair, yet he chose to find meaning in his life by becoming a powerful advocate for spinal cord injury research and accessibility. Through Dr. Frankl's lens, Reeve's hope wasn't in achieving physical recovery but in using his influence to impact the lives of others, creating purpose and connection even in the face of adversity. His journey shows us that hope, in Dr. Frankl's sense, is less about achieving certain outcomes and more about enduring with a sense of purpose. In finding ways to give back and deepen relationships, Reeve exemplified how we can hold on to meaning even when we can't control our circumstances.

Dr. Bandura and Dr. Snyder's Concept of Learned Hopefulness

Dr. Albert Bandura, renowned for his work in social learning and self-efficacy, provides a third perspective on hope, one that highlights our capacity to develop hopefulness as a learned skill. According to

Dr. Bandura, self-efficacy—the belief in one's ability to influence events and outcomes—is central to cultivating hope. When people perceive themselves as capable of overcoming challenges, they are more likely to set goals, persist through setbacks, and maintain a sense of hope even in adversity. Dr. Bandura argued that this belief in personal agency is not innate but can be nurtured through mastery experiences, social modeling, and positive feedback. In essence, hope is reinforced by the confidence gained from past successes and by observing others who achieve their goals. By developing self-efficacy, individuals cultivate the resiliency and optimism necessary to envision and work toward a better future, demonstrating that hope can be actively built through learning and experience.

Later adapted by Dr. Snyder, learned hopefulness is a concept that merges Dr. Bandura's self-efficacy with Dr. Snyder's understanding of hope, offering an empowering view: Hope can be cultivated, reinforced, and practiced.

Dr. Bandura's work on self-efficacy shows that when individuals experience even small successes, they gain confidence and motivation to continue pursuing their goals. Dr. Snyder incorporated this idea into hope theory, suggesting that hope grows through reinforcement and positive feedback. This concept helps us see hope as something that can be nurtured, built from the ground up, especially in environments that encourage us to believe in our own abilities.

Consider the story of Oprah Winfrey, who overcame a difficult childhood marked by poverty, abuse, and instability. Despite these hardships, Oprah found hope through teachers and mentors who celebrated her intelligence and resiliency. In her 2014 memoir *What I Know for Sure*, she shares that through their encouragement, she learned to see a future beyond her circumstances, internalizing a sense of worth and potential. This learned hopefulness guided her through years of hard work and self-belief, ultimately helping her to become one of the most influential media figures in the world. Oprah's story shows how hope, nurtured by positive reinforcement and supportive mentorship, can become a lifelong source of strength.

Similarly, the brilliant writer and thinker Maya Angelou's early life was filled with challenges, including trauma, displacement, and racial discrimination. Despite these experiences, Angelou found hope through mentors and advocates who recognized her talent and celebrated her writing and artistic gifts. Each positive reinforcement nurtured her sense of purpose, helping her see the possibility of a meaningful future. This learned hopefulness empowered her to pursue her voice as a poet, author, and civil rights activist, inspiring millions.

Another powerful example is that of Albert Einstein, who struggled academically in his early years and was even thought by some teachers to lack potential. However, with the encouragement of a few mentors who recognized his unique way of thinking, Einstein found hope in his ability to explore and ask questions. This positive reinforcement nurtured his curiosity, transforming self-doubt into confidence that helped him push the boundaries of science. His journey illustrates how learned hopefulness, supported by mentors who believe in us, can unlock extraordinary potential.

Finally, Helen Keller's story exemplifies the power of learned hopefulness. After losing her sight and hearing as a young child, Keller faced a world of isolation. Yet with the guidance of her teacher, Anne Sullivan, she learned to communicate and eventually excelled in her studies. Keller's learned hopefulness grew through Sullivan's encouragement, allowing her to see beyond her limitations. She went on to become a renowned author and activist, embodying how hope can grow with the right mentorship and support. Her journey shows us how resiliency and self-belief can flourish even in the most difficult circumstances.

Dr. Bandura's work on self-efficacy and Dr. Snyder's concept of learned hopefulness remind us that hope is not only a gift; it's a skill that grows over time with encouragement, positive experiences, and a network of supportive influences. When hope is nurtured in this way, it becomes a guiding force, helping us set goals, persevere, and believe in our capacity to shape our own lives.

Dr. Snyder, Dr. Frankl, and Dr. Bandura together offer us a rich, multidimensional view of hope. Hope can be a structured pathway toward our goals, a source of deep meaning in difficult times, and a skill that grows within us through practice and experience. As we reflect on our own lives, we can see that each perspective holds something valuable. In pursuing our goals, finding meaning in our struggles, and learning from each success and setback, we cultivate a form of hope that can sustain us. These stories show that when we choose to nurture hope, we arm ourselves with the courage to face whatever lies ahead, to act, to endure, and to connect with what truly matters. Hope is ultimately a commitment to life itself, a way of saying yes to possibility no matter how challenging the road.

Hope for a Friend, Hope for You

Sometimes it's hard to feel hopeful when we're stuck in our own heads. But something powerful happens when we take a step back and imagine how we'd support someone else in the same situation. This short exercise will help you tap into the natural hope, wisdom, and care you already offer others and see what it could feel like reflected back at you.

Think of a current challenge, setback, or hope you're holding right now. Now, imagine your best friend, your child, or even your puppy (Seriously, yes, even your puppy. I've given Apollo some pretty epic pep talks for not being intimidated by other dogs on our morning walks!) is facing the exact same situation.

Ask yourself:

- What would I say to them?
- How would I encourage them?
- What would I remind them about who they are?
- What is the one thing you would want to see them do?

Now flip it back to you:

- What happens when you offer that same support to yourself?
- How does it feel?
- Where do you feel it?
- What action does it inspire you to pursue?

Why This Works

This exercise taps into both agency and compassion, two pillars of hope theory. We're often much kinder, wiser, and more hopeful when it comes to others than we are to ourselves. But by shifting perspective, we access the part of us that *believes* change is possible. This inner coaching strategy is rooted in self-efficacy (Bandura), meaningful reframing (Frankl), and action-focused encouragement (Snyder). Sometimes, to find hope, we simply need to borrow our own voice of encouragement. When we learn to speak to ourselves the way we would to someone we care about, we don't just practice hope—we *become* the source of it.

5

Everyday Resiliency and the Hope Variable

> Let your hopes,
> not your hurts, shape
> your future.

ROBERT H. SCHULLER

I RELEASED MY FIRST BOOK, *Calm Within the Storm: A Pathway to Everyday Resiliency*, in the spring of 2021—almost a year to the date that COVID-19 was declared a global pandemic. The world was still locked down. I had spent months writing about human resiliency as people and the world appeared to be falling apart. My second book, *Stress Wisely: How to Be Well in an Unwell World*, launched in 2023 just as Freedom House announced, for the seventeenth straight year, that global freedom had declined.

This time around, as I write a book about hope, world tensions escalate in wars, AI offers promise and peril, and the heating temperature of the planet continues to shatter records. Seventy-nine million Americans are reeling from the latest election, the Israel-Hamas and Russia-Ukraine wars rage on, and the global life expectancy is declining for the first time in thirty years. So, if you're looking for the "right time" to do anything—go back to school, take that new job, talk with your elderly parents, buy that car, write that book—let me tell you, there's never a right time. Let that truth move you to action, not inaction. Make it the right time for you, because you decide that it's *your* time. I guarantee you, the world won't.

With the state of everything, how can we possibly be hopeful? This is where my work on everyday resiliency comes in. For those new to that work, here's a brief introduction. Think of this as the CliffsNotes version (or Coles Notes for my fellow Canadians!).

My theory of everyday resiliency was a culmination of nearly two decades of professional work and most of my personal life since as far back as I can remember. I've always been fascinated with the underdog. I wanted to know why, when life got hard, some people could get up while others would give up. I also wanted to know why and how I'd survived everything life had thrown at me thus far. I called my findings everyday resiliency because it's what we do each day that makes it possible to show up in every aspect of our lives.

I quickly learned that I would never meet a completely resilient person or a completely non-resilient person. People practice resiliency in different areas of their lives and under varying conditions. For example, you may be physically resilient—your body heals quickly and you're physically fit—yet struggle in situations that require emotional acuity and strength. Or a usually well-resourced person who is generally quite resilient might feel overwhelmed by everyday stressors after a poor night's sleep or a fight with a loved one. Resiliency isn't static but ever evolving.

Resiliency isn't just about bouncing back; it's about growing, learning, and unlearning how to show up. This is the big idea. What you do in ordinary time allows you to be extraordinary when called upon. It's building the capacity to weather life in a way that best serves you, your loved ones, and the greater good. Perhaps you become stronger, wiser, and more intentional, and that serves you well moving forward as you face more inevitable challenges. Or perhaps you become softer, gentler, and more compassionate in the face of life's hardships, with a deeper appreciation and understanding of the human condition and the fragility of life. My framework—which centers on the five pillars of belonging, perspective, acceptance, hope, and humor—offers a practical, relatable approach to cultivating resiliency. While each of these pillars support us in unique ways, hope plays a pivotal role as the most powerful element in building, practicing, and sustaining resiliency. But before we return to hope, let's set the stage with the other four pillars.

Belonging

While resiliency is often viewed as an individual strength, it's also deeply social. Belonging is the foundation that reminds us that we're not alone and we were never meant to navigate life that way.

The idea of being a lone wolf in hard times is a massive misconception. My work and the work of other researchers show that having someone in your corner is crucial for a person to weather life's challenges. For example, in child psychology there's an evaluation tool called ACEs, which stands for adverse childhood experiences. Research shows that when children are exposed to or experience certain events in childhood, they're more likely to have difficulty in adulthood. However, the same research demonstrates that one caring and consistent champion in a child's life can offer that child a hedge of protection, increasing the probability that the child will grow into a healthy adult. This adult could be a parent, grandparent, or even a coach or teacher. One person can make all the difference to a child's future.

Another example of how belonging impacts our behavior comes from a conversation I had with an old sea captain I met in Halifax. He shared that despite life vests being a regulation, he struggled to get his sailors to ever wear them. After yet another preventable tragedy at sea, while driving back to the harbor after informing the young wife that her husband was dead, the captain started a new protocol. He required each sailor to write the names of their loved ones with a Sharpie on the inside of their life vest. It radically changed life-vest compliance. Sometimes we change our behavior for ourselves, but more often, doing something for the people that are counting on us is the real game-changer.

One sailor told the captain that he really didn't have anyone's name to write. He had no family and no one for the captain to notify if he died. Remembering that the sailor had a dog, the captain told him he was pretty sure Buddy would like to have his supper, and that the sailor couldn't feed him from the bottom of the sea. The sailor grabbed the Sharpie and wrote "Buddy" in big, bold letters across his vest. "You know, Cap, that dog gets mad as hell if I'm late. Can't very well keep that boy waiting."

Perspective

In times of difficulty, perspective allows us to see beyond the immediate moment. It's the lens through which we view our experiences.

Our perspective grows in relation to our lived experiences. The more experiences we have, the greater the exposure to life, the deeper and broader the perspective. Developing and practicing an integrated perspective helps us manage challenges, mitigates the impact of stressors, and even offers the opportunity for learning and growth. This evolved way of seeing the world often starts with a perspective shift.

Side note: I absolutely love a mighty perspective shift. To me, it feels like a switch flips on or off, and I can never un-know or un-hear the new perspective moving forward. One of my favorite perspective shifts happened this past summer.

My son Hunter and I had traveled to Cincinnati to see Jaxson play in an Amateur Athletic Union basketball tournament—it's pretty amazing watching your kid do what they love and be part of something like that. Jaxson had traveled with the team, so Hunter and I went straight to the venue. After the team's warm-up, we saw Jaxson put on his tracksuit, take off his basketball shoes, and sit down on the bench. I asked Hunter why his brother wasn't playing, and he had no idea.

I decided to get to the bottom of this. I crossed that sacred threshold that separates fans from coaches, trainers, and athletes, and caught Jaxson's attention. I don't think the look on Jax's face was excitement, seeing me there in that moment. Jaxson informed me that he wasn't playing because he had left his dark jersey at the hotel room and the coach said no player plays if they forget any part of their uniform. I asked for the name of hotel, confident I could find it, get the jersey somehow, and be back by the second half. Jaxson reiterated, "The coach won't play me."

In that moment, I was experiencing a big feeling that high performers don't like to experience: helplessness. Give me anger, fear, sadness, or even jealousy and I'll use that as fuel, but helplessness? No, thank you. That's my kryptonite. When I returned to the stands, Hunter saw me upset and asked if he could offer me some advice.

Now, take a moment. I want to know, how open would you be to receiving advice from a twenty-year-old? You're feeling utterly helpless, you traveled all the way to Cincinnati to see your kid play, and he isn't playing simply because he forgot his jersey at the hotel. Despite all that, I leaned in to listen, and what Hunter said radically changed my perspective. "Mama, this is going to be a bad hour. It's not a bad day. It's not a bad tournament. And it's absolutely not a bad life. This is just going to be a bad hour, and you're just going to have to find a way just to sit with that, and, Mama, I promise you Jaxson will never forget a jersey again as long as he lives."

In that moment I had a perspective shift, and it really stuck. How often have I written off a day, a job, or a relationship as all bad or difficult when really it was just a bad hour? In this life, I promise you'll have many a bad hour, and my hope for you is that that one hour doesn't become a bad day.

Acceptance

As my bad-hour story illustrates a perspective shift, it also serves as an example of acceptance. Practicing acceptance daily is part of being resilient.

I say "daily" because acceptance isn't a one-and-done thing. It requires the ongoing commitment of working with your controllables—knowing what's within your control and what's outside your control. There's a tendency for us to spend more time thinking about what we don't have versus what we do have, or what we can't do versus what we can do. Having clarity about where you do have agency and influence helps.

A major barrier to acceptance is thinking that acceptance means approval or giving in. People tell me that if they accept whatever life circumstance they're dealing with, it would be a sign of weakness or an excuse. They just have to work harder. I totally get it. I fell into this faculty logic with my own mental health, learning disabilities, and ADHD. I spent most of my life fighting against the idea that my brain was wired differently than most people's. I thought I could out-work it. But no amount of lifestyle change—not even running 10K a day, an hour of yoga daily, a "clean" diet, or zero screen time—was ever going to change how ADHD impacted my thought processes and emotions. Yes, living a physically active lifestyle mitigated the symptoms for that period, but it didn't change the underlying experience.

I was shoveling while it was still snowing. And as soon as I let up, even an inch, I would be crushed by my reality once more. It was not sustainable for me to need over six hours a day of coping strategies just to be mildly okay. After decades of struggle, at my wits' end, I "succumbed" to medication for support. After my first dose, less than an hour after I took that one pill, I wept. I didn't know that feeling of clarity and calm existed. My world changed remarkably that day.

There's strength in surrender. Brighter tomorrows are possible with acceptance.

Humor

Fact: Resilient people are funny. And it's often a very dark sense of humor. I was perplexed by how many resilient people I worked with who also happened to be hilarious. How can people who go through such horrible things maintain a sense of humor despite it all?

At first, I thought humor was a deflection or defense mechanism. If anything got too serious or too difficult, resilient people would make an off-color comment or joke and keep moving forward. I quickly discovered that this tactic had a biological underpinning. For example, when people laugh, their bodies release a natural tranquilizer that blocks their pain receptors. You can't feel pain when you're laughing. Now, this doesn't solve the problem or the stressor, but it does provide a moment of reprieve so that the person can choose to respond versus react.

The ability to find humor lightens even the heaviest moments. Research also shows that laughter can be calming when you're scared. After confronting and dealing with a negative interaction, laughter can provide a release from the tension of the situation and return your nervous system to a calmer state.[1] I like to think that finding moments of humor or joy in the most absurd places while in a stressful situation is like activating psychological antibodies. The stress hormones are still present, but we just don't feel them as much. Having worked with members of the military, I can say with confidence that their superpower is humor. While there's obviously nothing funny about war or suffering, the way they use humor to maintain their humanity is remarkable. As one solider shared with me, "It's how you stay sane in the insane."

Humor is also a reliable strategy to de-escalate conflict and cut tension, easing people into more constructive and productive interactions. Authority figures who use humor effectively during a crisis are perceived by their organizations as being better leaders.[2] We can also observe humor as a means of shifting tension and distress into a more positive state for medical professionals, first responders, educators, and parents.

This healthy coping strategy has been around for a very long time. Historically, cracking jokes in this way was known as gallows humor; those on route to their demise would laugh and dance, often reinforcing claims of lunacy. Today we call it ER humor, or newsroom humor, or the military way. Most people find means of using humor to experience a moment of release from daily tensions, often in the form of memes, reels, or posts. When the sky is falling in your life, you might not be able to manage a conversation without crying your face off, but you can send that one meme that captures it all.

These four pillars of belonging, perspective, acceptance, and humor interweave to create a powerful foundation, each reinforcing the other with an undercurrent of hope that propels our lives forward. Now, let's dive deeper into how we can enhance these pillars with everyday hope practices that will absolutely enrich your life.

Everyday Resiliency at a Glance

Take a moment to capture your everyday resiliency pillars in four quick points. To deepen the impact, say your "I have," "I am," "I can," and "I will" statements out loud, write them in your journal, or post them somewhere visible—like your bathroom mirror or laptop screen. These aren't just words; they're anchors. Let them remind you of your capacity, your support, and your next right step.

- **I have** people in my corner who love me, support me, and stand by me even when I stumble. They won't let me fail at what matters most.

- **I am** well-resourced and capable of figuring things out. I am committed to showing up, even through the hard parts, because I matter, and I have the agency and ability to do whatever needs doing.

- **I can** do hard things. I can do great things. I can choose what happens next.

- **I will** take things one decision at a time, because you can only ever take things a moment at a time.

Why This Works

This exercise leverages principles from positive psychology and cognitive behavioral therapy to build emotional resiliency and mental strength. By affirming "I have," "I am," "I can," and "I will," you're actively engaging in cognitive restructuring, a proven technique to shift negative thinking patterns into positive, action-oriented mindsets.

These statements enhance self-efficacy by reinforcing a sense of capability and control. Acknowledging social support ("I have") and recognizing your inner resources ("I am") cultivates psychological safety and confidence, which are crucial for emotional well-being.

Repeating these affirmations—especially when spoken aloud or written down—also activates neuroplasticity, your brain's ability to rewire itself through experience and repetition. Each time you practice them, you help strengthen the neural pathways that support hope, confidence, and problem-solving. Over time, this repetition helps smooth and reinforce the myelin sheath around these pathways, making the messages easier for your brain to access under stress. In simple terms: The more you practice these beliefs, the more instinctively your brain can return to them when you need them most.

This approach also encourages psychological flexibility, enabling you to adapt to change and uncertainty more effectively. It promotes a balanced perspective: recognizing real challenges while affirming your ability to meet them. This mental framework not only reduces anxiety and stress, but also enhances self-trust, confidence, and the internal stability needed to keep going, even when the path ahead is hard. And, thankfully, you can do hard things!

6
From Hope to Resiliency

> I am not what happened to me; I am what I choose to become.

CARL JUNG

R: *HOPE IS omnipresent in each of the pillars of everyday resiliency, maybe not its own pillar, but part of all of them? Think on this more.*

Sitting in an Air Canada lounge while conducting my after-action report, this was my sticky note takeaway. (Yes, after each talk I spend a few minutes doing an after-action report even though I've delivered this material over 1,800 times. I'm committed to getting better every time. And, yes, I write on napkins or sticky notes, and yes, I address myself as "R" when assigning a job to myself.) My dear friend Phil M. Jones says it best: "Better beats best, every time." Reflecting after each repetition of doing whatever your thing is keeps you getting better.

As outlined in the previous chapter, hope has a presence in each of the pillars of everyday resiliency. Let's take a closer look at the mechanics for each to build our capacity to bring more hope into every aspect of our resiliency practices.

Hope and Belonging

Hope enhances our connections with others by fostering trust and mutual support. When we hold hope, we're more likely to reach out and build positive, constructive, and mutually beneficial relationships. Hope-driven belonging encourages us to lean on one another, reinforcing that we're stronger together. When we're hopefilled for others, and we can celebrate other people's wins and successes, we're able to foster deeper connections.

As Dr. Brené Brown writes, "Those who have a strong sense of love and belonging have the courage to be imperfect."[1] I believe that what other people may judge as imperfect or straying from the norm is often more in alignment with our most authentic self. And when you find your home team, the real people that matter, you won't be too much or too little of anything. With your people, you, just as you are, will be just right.

I recall being interviewed on a podcast near Valentine's Day. In the spirit of the season, the interviewer asked me how I knew my husband was "the one." Without skipping a beat, I said, "Because he's good for my nervous system." Probably not the most romantic response but definitely the truth. After a series of "lessons to be learned" relationships, which included betrayal beyond my wildest fears and a cruel family court nightmare that felt like I was part of the Salem witch hunt, my heart was battered and my trust in others was dismal. My sole focus was raising my three children to the best of my abilities. I embraced being a solo parent who was 100 percent responsible for everything. For those who ask if divorces are hard on children, they can be, but staying in dysfunctional relationships is much worse. You don't stay for the children's sake; you leave for your children's sake. I never imagined this as my reality. Nevertheless, I was committed to showing up each day as if my life and the lives of my children depended on it. Because they did.

Fast-forward to the day I realized I'd fallen head over feet, as in that famous Alanis Morissette song, in love with my best friend! Jeff, in his own way, healed four hearts that he never broke. He stepped up to raise three little ones as only he could. Jeff had already been riding alongside me as I navigated big seasons of trauma, grief, pain, and loss. He did it all while holding my hand. I can't stress enough that finding your people, be they partners or friends, gives you such an advantage for practicing resiliency. With the right people in your corner and as part of your community, you truly are unstoppable. You may not have found those relationships yet, and life may have taught you some pretty hard lessons, but do whatever you have to do to stay open to the possibility and opportunity for the right people to come into your life. It's remarkable how the right people can heal even the deepest wounds that may feel unhealable.

Perhaps you were neglected by your biological family, abandoned by your spouse, or bullied relentlessly in high school. Your past relationships don't have to spell a life sentence of living alone, relying on only yourself. We're designed to live in a community, but not just any community. Seek out the people who make your life safer and more secure. The right people for you are out there, and I believe they're just as excited to meet you as you'll be to meet them! The first step is knowing who you are and who you are not. Then, pay attention to who's around you when your nervous system settles and whose presence feels like coming home.

Hope and Perspective

Maintaining a hopeful perspective is essential, especially during challenging times. Hope helps us see beyond our immediate difficulties and keeps us focused on the potential for better outcomes. A hopeful perspective prevents us from falling into despair and keeps us engaged in finding solutions. It's protecting your head and heart from being pulled down into darkness or being driven by fear.

Imagine you're working with hundreds of school-age children, and your one job is to get their hopes up again. With the pandemic receding and children returning to school, some for the first time in two years, morale is low. Kindergarteners have missed some critical development lessons, such as sharing. Middle schoolers' emerging social skills have collapsed during online learning. High schoolers are years behind, socially and academically. Researchers have highlighted the potential enduring impact of COVID-19 on children in their research, for those interested in the full scope.[2]

I was one of these adults tasked with trying to rally our children and help them become more resilient. You may be wondering, How *do* you get children's hopes up again? I started with one question: What is the biggest, wildest, most special dream you can dream?

I prompted the children to imagine the coolest thing that could happen to them. I challenged even the adults in the room to get their hopes up again. One educator cautioned me that she didn't want the kids to get their hopes up—they'd already been through enough and she couldn't bear seeing them disappointed. I appreciate the sentiment, but that's faulty logic. We need children to use their imagination, creativity, and play to help heal.

One boy said the biggest dream he could imagine coming true was playing in the National Basketball Association (NBA). I loved this for him. I shared with him the names of tons of Canadian basketball players playing right now in the NBA, because representation and pathways matter. Heck, Jamal Murray grew up down the street from the school and just happened to have won the NBA Championship with the Denver Nuggets, making him the ninth Canadian do so.[3] I asked the boy what was one actionable step he could take on his dream pathway to playing in the NBA. "Maybe learn to play basketball, lady?"

Through a big smile, I told him that was a solid first step in the right direction. Amid our sweet exchange, with my new friend probably already preparing his draft speech—the light in his eyes told me that kid was making it happen—I noticed a boy in the crowd who looked less than pleased that his classmate was NBA-bound. "Hey, what's your deal?" I called to the boy. He reluctantly shared that he was disappointed his classmate's dream was coming true. I assured him that his mate hadn't been drafted yet and that he had a lot of work to put in first. I inquired as to why that made him angry. The boy shared with radical candor, "If that kid's dream comes true, mine won't."

Our world had been so ravaged by a scarcity and an us-versus-them mentality that this boy was convinced if something good happened to someone else, there wouldn't be any good left over for others. This belief isn't just common in schools. How often have you seen someone get a promotion, or meet an amazing partner, and the first thought isn't one of joy for them? You're absolutely not alone. When a scarcity mindset takes hold, it's hard to be happy for others or to believe there's enough to go around. I asked my angry little friend what his dream was. He said he wanted to be an astronaut. I jumped with enthusiasm and told him I'd recently shared a stage with Canadian legend Commander Chris Hadfield. I told the boy everything I could remember from Commander Hadfield's speech and from his book I read. The boy asked how Commander Hadfield became an astronaut. From what I remembered, he went into the Canadian Armed Forces, then to the Royal Military College of Canada, where he got a degree in mechanical engineering, and later went on to astronaut school at NASA. The once angry, now ecstatic young boy remarked, "Cool, just three things. I can do that!"

"Yes, you're not wrong, three things. I believe you can too," I replied. After the assembly, the well-intended educator asked me why I didn't correct the boy, because clearly becoming an astronaut takes more than just three things. "Because he is seven. It's time these kids got their hopes up again. We need them to dream it first." My gentle invitation, next time a child tells you they want to play in the National Hockey League or be a veterinarian or the first Indigenous prime minister or president, tell them you believe in them. The world has a way of course-correcting in due time, but there's nothing wrong with setting a dream ablaze. Some sparks will catch, and the world will be better for it.

Hope and Acceptance

Hope also shapes how we accept our circumstances. Acceptance doesn't mean resignation; it's about acknowledging reality while still believing in the possibility of positive change. Hope within acceptance allows us to face difficult truths without losing sight of our potential to grow and adapt. I think of hope and acceptance like a shield and a path. We work with our controllables in an honest way while staying committed to our course.

In a shocking moment during an NFL Monday Night Football game on January 2, 2023, Buffalo Bills safety Damar Hamlin collapsed on the field after suffering a cardiac arrest following a routine tackle. The incident unfolded in front of a packed stadium and millions watching live, sending waves of fear and uncertainty across the sports world. Medical personnel immediately administered CPR and used a defibrillator to restore his heartbeat on the field before transporting him to a nearby hospital. The game was suspended and later canceled, a rare move underscoring the gravity of the situation. The episode sparked an outpouring of support and hope from fans, players, and communities across the globe. Hamlin's family, teammates, and the NFL leaned on hope during his critical condition, which gradually improved due to the swift response of medical teams. His recovery became a symbol of resiliency and inspired countless acts of generosity, including donations to Hamlin's charitable foundation. The incident underscored the importance of acceptance in the face of uncertainty and tragedy. For those on the field and in the audience, accepting the gravity of Hamlin's condition was a painful but necessary step to focus on his recovery and well-being. Acceptance allowed individuals and communities to channel their emotions productively, whether through prayer, financial contributions, or expressions of solidarity. Simultaneously, hope played a pivotal role. It kept fans, teammates, and the broader sports world united in optimism during a time of profound vulnerability. Hamlin's eventual return to health served as a testament to the power of hope, the effectiveness of modern medicine, and the impact of collective compassion. His journey highlighted how acceptance and hope can coexist, offering strength in times of crisis and paving the way toward healing.

Another powerful example of hope and acceptance working together came during the early days of the COVID-19 pandemic. Across the world, people masked, social distanced, and dramatically altered their lives—not out of panic, but out of community care and a shared belief that collective action could lead to recovery. It was a global moment of accepting difficult circumstances while holding tightly to hope—the hope that our sacrifices could save lives, protect the vulnerable, and help us move through uncertainty together. That kind of coordinated compassion reminded us that even in isolation, hope can be deeply communal.

In the film *Cast Away*, hope and acceptance are also poignantly illustrated through Tom Hanks's character, Chuck Noland. Stranded on a desert island, he forms a deep emotional bond with Wilson, a volleyball turned companion. Wilson isn't just a makeshift friend—he represents belonging and the human need for connection. That relationship, though entirely imagined, gives Chuck the hope and emotional anchor he needs to survive.

But hope wasn't found only in Wilson—it was carried also in the form of a single FedEx package Chuck refused to open. That package gave him a sense of purpose, a tether to the world beyond the island. Even though he had no idea what was inside, he preserved it and ultimately delivered it after his rescue. The delivery itself didn't change the world, and he never met the recipient. But the act of holding on to that purpose—of believing it still mattered—helped him stay connected to a future beyond his current suffering. In that story, we see that even imagined connection and simple acts of meaning can serve as powerful vehicles for hope.

Hope and Humor

Finally, hope allows us to embrace humor and joy as coping mechanisms. Hope helps us find lightness in heavy situations and lets us laugh even in times of stress. When we have hope, humor becomes a tool that empowers us to face hardship with resiliency. Hope and humor are complementary sides of an experience, offering a way to face life's difficulties with strength and perspective. Hope keeps us moving forward, with a view to a brighter horizon even when the road is hard, while humor lightens the journey, offering moments of levity that remind us of our humanity. Together, they form a resilient pairing, helping us navigate the darkest times with courage and wit. Humor, especially when paired with hope, doesn't diminish the seriousness of challenges; it equips us to endure them. It shows us that even when we can't control our circumstances, we can choose our attitude.

Take, for instance, Winston Churchill, a leader who exemplified the union of hope and humor in times of crisis. During World War II, with the weight of a nation's survival on his shoulders, Churchill is famously attributed with saying, "If you're going through hell, keep going" (though according to the International Churchill Society, he never actually said this).[4] Regardless, this simple, almost wry statement brims with hope and defiance. Humor doesn't make the flames of adversity less real, but it reminds us to press on, to focus on the possibility of emerging stronger on the other side. Churchill's humor reflected not just a personal philosophy but a way of rallying others, infusing hope into the hearts of those who might otherwise have succumbed to despair. Similarly, Churchill quipped, "For my part, I consider that it will be found much better by all parties to leave the past to history, especially as I propose to write that history myself." Again, the sentiment remains true. This remark, while amusing, is a lesson in shaping one's narrative with hope and agency. Leaders in any context, military, political, or even within families, can learn from this approach. Humor acknowledges the challenge, hope sees the possibility of triumph, and together they inspire action. In moments of great adversity, hope peppered with humor doesn't erase the struggle, but rather offers moments of reprieve so we can endure and persist through any storm. Because the reality is that none of us are making it out of this alive. We might as well make the best of it.

By acknowledging, integrating, and cultivating hope across each pillar, we build a more adaptable, enduring form of resiliency that carries us through both daily challenges and major life events. No pillar operates without some degree of hope. Whether fostering belonging, shaping our perspectives, guiding our acceptance, or enabling us to find humor in adversity, hope serves as both an anchor and a catalyst. It connects us to others, helps us navigate challenges, and inspires us in even the most daunting circumstances to dream beyond what may seem possible.

Each story and reflection in this chapter demonstrates that hope is not passive. It's an active, vibrant force that propels us forward. From strengthening our connections to others to helping us find lightness amid difficulties, hope equips us with the mindset and energy needed to persevere. In fostering resiliency, hope allows us to embrace life fully, not as a series of insurmountable obstacles, but as a journey where we grow stronger, kinder, and more capable of achieving what matters most.

A Hopeful Check-In

You can quickly assess and cultivate hope in your daily life by identifying small, actionable steps to reduce stress and build resiliency. This exercise is designed to be simple, taking just a few minutes, and can be done anytime you feel overwhelmed or stuck.

Step 1: Pause and Reflect

Take a deep breath and ask yourself: "Where am I feeling the most stress right now?"

Identify one area of your life that feels heavy or challenging (e.g., work, relationships, health, finances). Notice what is within your control, somewhat within your control, and outside of your control. Pick one area that is within your control or somewhat within your control to take to step 2.

Step 2: Hopeful Reframe

Ask yourself: "What is one small thing I can do to feel a little more hopeful about this situation?"

This could be as simple as sending an encouraging text to a friend for social support, taking a ten-minute walk to clear your mind, making a list of small, manageable tasks to reduce overwhelm, or practicing gratitude by writing down one thing that's going well.

Step 3: Anchor in Hope

Finish by saying to yourself: "I don't have to solve everything right now. I just need to take one small step toward hope."

Visualize how taking this small step might create a positive ripple effect in your life.

Reflection Questions
- How did identifying a small, hopeful action shift your perspective?
- What emotions did you notice before and after the exercise?
- How can you incorporate this practice into your daily routine?

Why This Works

This exercise uses cognitive behavioral techniques to interrupt negative thought patterns and introduce solution-focused thinking. By focusing on small, actionable steps, you engage in pathways thinking—a key component of hope theory—which helps you identify multiple routes to your goals, reducing feelings of helplessness.

By grounding the practice in the present moment, this exercise also leverages mindfulness-based stress reduction, helping you break the cycle of rumination and fostering emotional resiliency. This simple approach cultivates psychological flexibility and empowers you to navigate stress with a renewed sense of hope and agency.

7

Stress Wisely with a Dose of Hope

> You may encounter many defeats, but you must not be defeated. In fact, it may be necessary to encounter the defeats, so you can know who you are.

MAYA ANGELOU

IF YOU'RE LIKE most people, you've tried at one point or another to change your behavior, likely with varying degrees of success. The reality is that all humans are in a constant state of change and adaption. Even the practice of trying not to change is what psychologists call a "change state." Resisting change, or not changing, is itself a change state because it represents an active decision to maintain the current condition amid evolving circumstances, thereby altering the natural flow of adaptation. You want to know what's scarier than change? Staying the same. Not having the agency to change is terrifying. Imagine having to stay exactly the same, in every area of your life, as you are right now in perpetuity! No, thank you!

While some behaviors are adaptive and move you closer to your goals, other behaviors are maladaptive and lead you further away, but no matter what direction, all human behaviors serve a purpose. There's a tension between where you are and where you're going; who you are and who you're becoming. From an evolutionary perspective, our ability to change is critical for our survival despite our very fractured relationship with change and behavior modification. As a trained behaviorist, I've worked everywhere from labs with rats to maximum-security prisons, from sports venues to classrooms, stages, and boardrooms. And what I love about this field of psychology is that the principles of behaviorism are consistent. The rules that explain how we change, or better yet, struggle with change, are solid. Dr. Ivan Pavlov and Dr. B. F. Skinner sure got behavioral and operant conditioning right!

You might be wondering what all this has to do with hope. Here's the point: As I worked with people from all walks of life in different settings, I appreciated that people had varying degrees of understanding about behavioral principles and the role of hope in choosing how we act, respond, or even attribute outcomes.

Take success, for example. Some people would attribute success to things like luck or chance, while other people recognized success as commitment, dedication, consistency, and clarity of goals. Or when it came to athletic excellence, some attributed wins to genetics and who they knew, while others could see how lifestyle choices and hours in the gym and on the field led to their greatness.

This difference was evident also in how people approached their own well-being. I noticed first that a lot of people didn't practice resiliency principles and associated behaviors for resiliency's sake; instead, they attempted to get out of difficulties, challenges, or hardships. Now, there was a remarkable difference in how people approached longer-term wellness versus just wanting to feel different. Some engaged in behaviors because they wanted to feel better, while others just wanted to feel something else—anything else, really. I would see this in their choice of behaviors, and those behaviors had a lot to do with their thoughts and feelings. For example, let's say someone is experiencing a stressful situation at work. Person 1 shares their troubles with a loved one, goes for walks on their lunch hour, and updates their résumé so that when opportunity knocks, they're ready. Person 2 suffers alone, spends their lunch hour mindlessly scrolling for digital dopamine, and feels helpless to do anything about their circumstances. Or let's say two people are experiencing an injury. Person 1 listens to their healthcare providers, accepts that they can't heal overnight, and follows through with their physio exercises. (Side note: Research shows that only about 35 to 50 percent of physiotherapy patients fully adhere to their prescribed home exercise programs![1]) Person 2 treats their body like an old car, decides its time is up and they aren't sinking any more time, money, energy or effort into it, and lets it rust out. I also learned that how people behaved in relation to their stressors radically improved their ability to be resilient. I then dived into what areas of focus provided the best return on their investment. From that work came my 2023 book *Stress Wisely*.

Stressing wisely isn't about getting rid of stress in your life, because frankly, that's impossible. As a therapist once told me, trying to achieve a stress-free life is a dead-man's goal! Our stress system, also known as our nervous system, isn't our enemy but rather our greatest ally. It's a remarkable first line of defense. When we work with our nervous system, not against it, people can be truly well even in the most remarkable circumstances. As I researched *Stress Wisely*, I noticed how hope and hope-fueled behaviors impacted the way people showed up in every area of their lives. The capacity to choose and change our behaviors (opting for more hopefilled well-being practices) as well as self-attribution (being willing work for better outcomes) were at the heart of stressing wisely.

Hope became the main character in my work on resiliency and well-being, touching each domain of my stressing wisely model. In that model, I outlined the eight realms of wellness: physical, emotional, intellectual, social, environmental, occupational, financial, and spiritual. These domains represent the diverse ways we experience and respond to stress, with hope, inspired behaviors, and action weaving into the unifying thread that strengthens them all. Just as the previous chapters connected the practice of everyday resiliency with hope, this chapter will give stressing wisely some love and airtime too.

Every Domain Gets a Shot of Hope

The **physical** domain, the foundation of our well-being, is deeply influenced by hope. When illness or injury strikes, hope sustains us, reminding us that recovery is possible. Research in psychoneuroimmunology underscores this connection: Individuals with higher levels of hope often recover faster and adhere more consistently to treatment plans.[2] Take, for instance, a woman named Claire who faced a cancer diagnosis. The journey through chemotherapy was grueling, but Claire's hope for a life beyond cancer kept her going, especially the drive to be there for her young boys. She found ways to celebrate even the smallest victories, such as finishing a treatment cycle or maintaining her appetite for a day, and these moments of progress reinforced her belief that she'd have a big, bright cancer-free future, and her boys would have their mom. Another woman I worked with struggled deeply with feeling betrayed by her body when she received a second cancer diagnosis. Her body-hatred polluted every aspect of her treatment and despair took hold. Her family watched helplessly as their beloved mother lost the will to fight.

Hope also plays a critical role in preventive health. It inspires people to engage in behaviors that promote physical well-being and safety, from eating nourishing foods and making time for daily movement to putting on a seat belt, practicing safer sex, and even changing batteries in smoke alarms. People engage in pro-health behaviors because they believe they work. You take medication hoping it'll relieve the pain. You get your seven-to-eight hours of sleep the night before a big presentation. By cultivating hope within the physical realm, we choose to believe that these behaviors will get us closer to our goals of feeling good today and in the future. I remember hearing an interview with Dr. Peter Attia, the author of *Outlive*, who listed physical things we need to do now in order to be able to do them in the future. One example was to carry 75 percent of your body weight in free weights, for sixty seconds, and if you could do that at forty-five years old, you'd be able to open a jar at ninety years old. As a forty-five-year-old, I thought that sounded pretty good. I went to our home gym to test it out. At dinner, I proudly shared with the family that I'd be able to open jars when I'm ninety years old because I'd successfully held 75 percent of my body weight, in a farmer hold, for sixty seconds. To my surprise, they all started laughing. When I asked what was so funny, Jaxson replied, "Mama, you can't open jars now." Practice makes better, right? Our physical well-being is a practice. Everyday decisions count and so does hope.

In the **emotional** domain, hope acts as an anchor, steadying us through life's storms. Emotions are fluid, and in times of grief, anxiety, or uncertainty, it can feel like we're adrift. Hope provides the buoyancy we need to stay afloat. Research highlights that hope buffers against depression and anxiety, offering a pathway to emotional stability.[3] I recall meeting a man named Dan who had recently lost his wife. The weight of grief threatened to overwhelm him, but he found hope in small rituals: walking their favorite path in the park, journaling his memories, and envisioning a future where he could honor her by living fully. Hope didn't erase his pain, but it did allow him to navigate it, offering a lifeline that pulled him toward healing. I connected deeply with Dan's pain as someone who also has experienced life-altering grief.

My mother was my everything. Everything good in my life was connected to her and was because of her. Grief rewrites us, and we never actually get over it. Time doesn't heal; rather, it helps us get better at carrying our grief wherever we go. When I'm feeling like the grief is particularly difficult to carry, I try to do one thing that I know for certain she would do. Maybe it's sending a card, or making the children cookies, or feeding the pets something extra-special. I remember visiting my mom at the lake house and being met with the smell of butter and garlic at the door. I commented that something smelled good, and she told me that this round of roasted garlic shrimp was for her cat, but she would be happy to make me some after she served Tigger. (Note: Please don't feed your cats garlic, but do channel my mother's joie de vivre!) Small practices done with intention can help us believe that the wave of sadness will once again recede, and we can soften the edges of our pain. Practices like these help us feel close to our loved ones, cultivating a sense of hope that our connection still exists, albeit in a much different way.

Hope is equally vital in the **intellectual** domain, where growth, learning, and problem-solving reside. Challenges in this domain—whether mastering a new skill or facing a difficult decision—can feel daunting, but hope fuels perseverance. A group of UK researchers found that hope is a strong predictor of academic success, as it fosters both motivation and resiliency. They went on to explain that hope uniquely predicted objective academic achievement above IQ, personality, and previous school achievement.[4] I once worked with a young refugee who was learning English as a second language while juggling a low-paying job and children. The frustration of slow progress often tempted her to give up, but her hope for a better future for her children kept her engaged. She believed that learning English would open more opportunities for them all. She celebrated small achievements, like holding her first conversation with a coworker, and used those victories to fuel her belief in her ability to succeed. Hope helps us reconstruct challenges as being worth it. It allows people to see opportunities for growth, encouraging us to persist and adapt. By focusing on the steps we can take rather than the obstacles in our way, we cultivate intellectual well-being. Our circumstances are not characteristics. The hope lies in our ability to change, grow, learn, and even unlearn what no longer serves us.

In the **social** domain, hope strengthens our connections with others. Relationships are often tested by conflict, distance, or misunderstandings, but hope allows us to believe in the possibility of reconciliation and deeper connection. There's a popular reel on social media that states that true friendships resist time, distance, and silence. Research published in the *Journal of Social and Personal Relationships* demonstrates that hope fosters trust and positive communication, even during challenging times.[5] I remember facilitating a workshop for a group of colleagues who'd experienced a workplace conflict. Initially, tensions were high, but through guided discussions and shared goals, hope began to emerge. One participant expressed a belief that the team could rebuild trust, and that simple act of hope became contagious. By the end of the workshop, the group had developed a renewed commitment to collaboration. In our personal lives, hope encourages us to reach out, repair relationships, and build new ones. Acts of kindness, empathy, and active listening are ways to nurture hope in the social domain, reminding us that even in isolation, we aren't truly alone.

The **environmental** domain encompasses the spaces and places we inhabit, from our homes to the natural world. Hope in this domain empowers us to take responsibility for our surroundings, transforming them into sources of resiliency. Environmental psychology highlights the role of hope in promoting sustainable behaviors, such as reducing waste or conserving energy. I remember working with a group of forest firefighters from Northern Alberta and British Columbia. One recruit explained how they were tasked with a tree-planting initiative in a wildfire-ravaged area. He held out a tiny sapling to me. "I won't ever see her grow into much, but I sure hope someone's kid does."

On a personal level, hope in the environmental domain might look like creating a calming space in your home or finding moments of peace in nature. We'll dive into this more later. These choices remind us that we have the power to shape our environments in ways that support our well-being.

The **occupational** domain, encompassing both our paid and unpaid work, is another area where hope is transformative. Work can be a source of stress, especially when the demands placed on us exceed our capacity or when we feel unfulfilled. Hope, however, provides perspective and purpose, reminding us of the value of our contributions. Research in organizational behavior shows that hopeful employees are more engaged and resilient, and hopeful leaders inspire innovation and collaboration. During a leadership seminar, I met a nurse who worked in a high-stress intensive care unit. Despite the challenges, she found hope in the stories of recovery she witnessed and in the camaraderie of her team. She described hope as "the thing that keeps me showing up, even on the hard days." By focusing on the impact of her work, Rachel turned a stressful job into a source of meaning and purpose.

Whether through career transitions, leadership roles, or everyday tasks, hope in the occupational domain fuels our motivation and sustains our efforts. One of my most interesting findings when researching this domain was the power of the noble pursuit. Keeping an eye on how their role plays into a greater purpose offers a person in a difficult job a hedge of protection around the stressors of that job. An example is the mom who worked three low-paying jobs to support her kids and found the stress navigable because she knew it provided for her family. Or the operator in the military who told me he was doing one of the worst military jobs imaginable, knowing someone else didn't have to.

Financial stress, a common source of anxiety, is profoundly influenced by hope. The financial domain isn't just about resources; it's about our ability to manage uncertainty and plan for the future. Studies in behavioral finance reveal that hope promotes positive financial behaviors, such as saving for emergencies and pursuing long-term goals. Research published in the *American Journal of Lifestyle Medicine* further highlights that incorporating hope theory into financial education and coaching programs significantly enhances individuals' sense of hopefulness, which in turn fosters consistent saving, prudent spending, and long-term financial planning.[6] Why? Because hope encourages us to envision a better future and believe in our ability to achieve it. When people feel hopeful, they're more likely to set long-term goals, such as saving for emergencies or retirement, because they see a positive outcome as attainable. This optimistic outlook enhances motivation and self-discipline, making it easier to delay gratification and prioritize future needs over immediate desires. Additionally, hope fosters resiliency, helping individuals persist in their financial goals even when faced with setbacks or economic uncertainty. In this way, hope not only shapes financial decisions, but also sustains the commitment needed to achieve long-term financial security.

I recall a single mother who was determined to buy a home for her children despite limited income. Hope gave her the dedication to stick to a budget, seek financial counseling, and celebrate milestones along the way. Each small success reinforced her belief in her ability to achieve her goal. Hope in the financial domain increases our agency to do something about our current situations. By focusing on what we can control, we cultivate financial empowerment.

One of my dearest friends, financial superhero Jillian Carr, radically transformed my financial well-being by helping me realize that I wasn't alone in my own financial wilderness. I'm someone who oscillates between save for the future and you only live once, and I ebb and flow between those two philosophies on the daily. I thought people were all one or the other—go figure! Through education and a solid plan, my dual-truth approach made room for hope: People like me can enjoy the nice things today and have confidence in their future too.

Finally, the **spiritual** domain weaves through all aspects of our lives, offering a profound sense of meaning and connection that transcends daily challenges. Hope in this domain fosters trust in the journey and belief in the possibility of transformation, even in the face of profound adversity. Research published in the *Journal of Religion and Health* emphasizes that spiritual hope reduces existential anxiety, strengthens resiliency, and promotes well-being by helping individuals navigate life's complexities with peace and clarity.[7]

A compelling real-world example of spiritual hope is Nelson Mandela's story during his twenty-seven years of imprisonment. Despite the harsh conditions and the seeming impossibility of overcoming apartheid in South Africa, Mandela's spiritual hope kept him grounded. Drawing strength from his belief in justice and humanity's capacity for change, he maintained a vision of a united and free South Africa. Mandela once said, "I am fundamentally an optimist. Whether that comes from nature or nurture, I cannot say. Part of being optimistic is keeping one's head pointed toward the sun, one's feet moving forward."[8] While in prison, Mandela engaged in acts of reflection, prayer, and service, such as teaching fellow inmates and mediating conflicts, which strengthened his hope and sustained his purpose. His unwavering spiritual hope became a source of strength for not only himself but also millions of South Africans who looked to him as a symbol of resiliency and the possibility of transformation. After his release, Mandela's hope-fueled leadership helped guide South Africa toward reconciliation and democracy, demonstrating how spiritual hope can inspire profound change and collective healing. Mandela's story reminds us that hope in the spiritual domain connects us to something larger than ourselves, empowering us to find meaning in adversity and inspiring others to do the same. It's a testament to how hope and spirituality can guide us through life's darkest moments toward transformation and renewal.

Another powerful example of spiritual hope can be found in the life and philosophy of Dr. Stephen

Hawking, the renowned theoretical physicist and cosmologist. Diagnosed with ALS at the age of twenty-one and given only a few years to live, Dr. Hawking faced the devastating prospect of progressive paralysis. Yet instead of succumbing to despair, he found purpose and meaning in exploring the mysteries of the universe. Dr. Hawking's spiritual hope was rooted in his awe and wonder at the cosmos, his quest to understand the nature of existence, and his commitment to advancing human knowledge.

He once remarked, "However difficult life may seem, there is always something you can do and succeed at. It matters that you don't just give up."[9] His hope was not based on religious faith but on a profound connection to science, curiosity, and the potential of human intellect. Despite his physical limitations, Dr. Hawking continued to contribute groundbreaking work in physics, write bestselling books, and inspire millions with his vision of the universe and his courage in the face of adversity. His life illustrates that spiritual hope can be anchored in a secular, existential search for meaning and a sense of purpose that transcends personal suffering.

Across these eight domains, hope and hope-fueled behaviors are the threads that bind each realm of wellness to true well-being and resiliency. While hope doesn't eliminate challenges, it equips us to face them with courage, creativity, and compassion. Hope transforms adversity into opportunity, connection into strength, and setbacks into stepping stones. By intentionally cultivating hope in these eight domains, we create a life that's rich, balanced, and resilient. As you reflect on these domains, consider where hope is most active in your life and where it might need nurturing. By embracing hope as a foundation for resiliency and well-being, you not only sustain yourself but inspire those around you, creating a ripple effect of possibility and strength—which is exactly what the world needs most right now.

Hope Mapping for Stress Resiliency

Grab a pen and paper for this one! This exercise is designed to help you consciously integrate hope into each domain of your life, supporting you in stressing wisely and enhancing your overall well-being. By mapping out where hope currently exists and where it needs nurturing, you can build a personalized strategy for resilient living.

Insights and Mapping

Draw a big circle and divide it into eight segments, each representing one of the wellness realms: physical, emotional, intellectual, social, environmental, occupational, financial, and spiritual.

In each segment, answer the following questions:

1 Where in this domain do you already feel hopeful or optimistic? (For example, in the physical domain, you might feel hopeful about reaching a fitness goal.)

2 Where do you feel stuck, overwhelmed, or hopeless? (For example, in the financial domain, you may feel uncertain about debt.)

3 What is one hopeful action you can take to enhance your sense of agency and possibility?

Visualization and Affirmation

Close your eyes and visualize each domain flourishing with hope. Imagine the ripple effect of this hope impacting your life positively.

Repeat a personalized affirmation for each domain. Example: "I am capable of nurturing hope in my emotional well-being, and I am open to healing and growth."

Action and Accountability

Choose one hopeful action from any domain to implement this week. Share your plan with someone who supports you to increase accountability. Becoming a hope-dealer is a thing. You become the person who talks about hope, inspiring others to be more hopefilled too.

Reflection Questions

In which domain do you feel the strongest sense of hope? Why?

In which domain is hope the most challenging for you? What barriers are present?

How does acknowledging hope (or the lack of it) shift your perspective on stress?

What supportive resources or people can help you maintain hope in challenging domains?

Why This Works

This exercise is rooted in hope theory, which emphasizes the importance of goal-setting, pathways thinking, and agency in fostering hope. By identifying areas where hope is present or needed, you are engaging in cognitive restructuring, a technique used in cognitive behavioral therapy to reframe negative thought patterns into positive, action-oriented narratives.

The process of mapping hope across wellness domains enhances psychological flexibility and emotional resiliency as it encourages you to recognize challenges while actively seeking solutions. By visualizing hopeful outcomes and taking small, meaningful actions, you strengthen self-efficacy—the belief in your ability to influence events and outcomes.

Additionally, asking hard questions and confronting areas of hopelessness promotes emotional intelligence and self-awareness, allowing you to break free from limiting beliefs and build a more resilient mindset. This approach not only reduces anxiety but also fosters a sense of purpose and optimism, empowering you to stress wisely with a dose of hope.

8

The Evolution of Hope Across Life's Seasons

> # Out of your vulnerabilities will come your strength.
>
> **DR. SIGMUND FREUD**

HAVE YOU EVER WONDERED who the "real you" actually is? Is the real you the one who sets the alarm the night before for 6 a.m., or the one at 6 a.m. who hits snooze and goes back to sleep?

You're not alone. I like to think that it's motivation that sets the alarm and discipline that gets us out of bed. Similar to how motivation and discipline are complementary forces that ebb and flow, I believe that hope ebbs and flows at different points along an experience. In the previous chapters, we examined how our practices of everyday resiliency and stressing wisely were interconnected with hope. In this chapter, we will take a closer look at how hope adapts at different points along the way.

Hope looks different as we move through the seasons of our lives. In beginnings, hope fuels dreams and possibilities. In middles, it sustains us through complexities and challenges. In endings, it offers peace and reflection, helping us find meaning and closure. By understanding how hope evolves in these seasons, we can better nurture it and apply it as a force for resiliency and well-being in our lives.

Hopeful Beginnings: Building Dreams and Possibilities

My "new year" season starts in September when school is back in session. I appreciate that many people celebrate New Year's in January, but for me, the new school year gleams with possibilities, the comfort of returning to familiar routines, and the wonder of crisp autumn days. Mind you, it's not all magical; it *is* also the season of making school lunches again. Probably one of the only elements of raising school-age children I absolutely don't miss!

Hope almost seems plentiful in the beginning. Of course, there may be some nervous excitement or anticipation, yet hope seems to steady the waves of newness. I remember when Hunter was starting high school and was nervous about making the leap. Having just read the book *We Bought a Zoo*, I borrowed some parenting prowess from one of my new favorite quotes: "You know, sometimes all you need is twenty seconds of insane courage, just literally twenty seconds of embarrassing bravery, and I promise you something great will come of it."[1] Thank you, Benjamin Mee! After Hunter's first day, he remarked that he actually needed multiple sets of twenty seconds of insane courage, but it worked out.

I kid you not, two years later when Ava was starting high school, Hunter shared with the family what had actually happened on his first day. Hunter was walking down the main staircase that connected the atrium to the cafeteria, and in front of "the entire school," he fell headfirst down a concrete set of stairs. Just as he was about to smash his face at the bottom, a senior student he happened to play basketball with caught him. Nate put Hunter promptly back on his feet and told him that first step was a tricky one. "Watch where you're going, Huncho, we need you on the court this season." Shocked, grateful, and confused, I asked why he didn't tell me. "I knew you would call Nate's mom and make a big deal of it." Hunter wasn't wrong! Despite a few bumps, waves of nervousness, and potentially a trip down the stairs, in the beginning hope carries us through, with perhaps a little help from a friend and a good book too.

Hope is often most vibrant and expansive in the early stages of a journey. Beginnings are characterized by curiosity, excitement, and a sense of possibility. Whether we're starting a new career, moving to a new city, beginning a relationship, or launching a personal project, hope propels us forward. It inspires us to dream big, set goals, and step into the unknown with courage.

For a little one starting their first day of school, hope might look simple, like meeting a friend, learning something exciting, or showing off their new indoor shoes! These small yet significant hopes shape how children approach new environments. Hope helps them embrace challenges and develop the resiliency they'll carry into teenagerhood and adulthood. Hope activates initiative and increases the opportunity to learn, adapt, and grow.

For adults, beginnings often come with a mix of excitement and apprehension. I recall leaving a weekend Costco run with two of my teenagers in tow, and a woman with her own set of teenagers stopped us, politely but with great enthusiasm. I'd never met the woman before, but she asked me if I was Robyne, then introduced me to her teenagers as the reason she left her job as an educator! "After hearing Dr. Robyne at a board event, I bought her book and then made the decision to quit my job as an educational assistant. I went back to school to become a dental hygienist, because that's the profession I always wanted but was pressured to go into education."

The woman's teenage daughter looked at me in surprise and hugged me. "Thank you for inspiring my mom. She's so much happier now. She's the happiest I've ever seen her and has an amazing job. I always wanted to meet you and say thank you." WOW. In that moment, I was speechless. Standing in a parking lot now since we were holding up the line, this brave, bold, and confident woman recounted to me the apprehension of leaving her steady job but also the excitement of choosing to bet on herself.

My dear friend Natalie Davison shared with me an insight recently that captures this experience: "The transformation happens at the transaction." This woman experienced a transformation the moment she left her job, not only for herself but also for her family. She felt the fear *and* the excitement, and did it anyway.

But beginnings aren't always easy. The unknown can feel overwhelming, and failures may seem particularly discouraging in these early stages. This is where hope becomes a stabilizing force, reminding us that setbacks are part of the process. A friend of mine once described her early parenting experiences as a whirlwind of joy and exhaustion. "I hoped I was doing it right," she said, reflecting on the countless decisions that come with raising a child. Her hope wasn't in achieving perfection but in trusting that love and effort would guide her family toward connection and growth. As I told her, if you're asking yourself whether you're a good parent, you're already an excellent one. The bad ones don't ask that question!

Nurturing hope in beginnings requires flexibility and openness with your feelings. While you celebrate small victories, embrace curiosity, and allow yourself to adapt, also recognize that being a beginner or even the underdog is an amazing place to start from. Personally, my favorite place to operate from professionally is as the rookie in the situation. I've shown up in a multitude of professional situations comparable to fighting above my weight class. I love knowing that most people who hear me speak for the first time onstage haven't heard of me yet, so they don't have any expectations. I believe in my skills, talents, and gifts enough to take the risk of walking out there knowing I'll inevitably connect with one person who needs to hear what I'm there to say, and that's all that matters. Beginnings are an opportunity to imagine, explore, dream, stretch, and build, with hope as your compass.

Hopeful Middles: Sustaining Momentum and Navigating Complexity

The middle seasons of life often present a unique set of challenges. Whether in careers, relationships, long-term projects, or personal growth, the middle can feel like an endless balancing act. I think of hope in the middle season as mile 10 in the 13.1-mile race. I freaking hate mile 10, in every race, a lot. I recall running in a half-marathon race in Florida and feeling fantastic. My strides were smooth, the breathing steady, my mind calm, and I thought for a moment that maybe, just maybe, the training leading up to this race would see me through. In full disclosure, I may have shown up for a bunch of half-marathons with little to no training, which would explain why when I hit mile 10, I was usually cooked. But this time, since I had trained, I'd fooled myself into believing that training would prevent me from hitting the mile 10 wall. I was confident in this belief until I saw the mile 10 sign and BAM. Just like Wile E. Coyote being taken out by a boulder from that bully the Road Runner, as soon as my brain saw that marker, everything seized. My legs felt like I was running with concrete shoes. I was wheezing like a pack-a-day smoker. My mind panicked. And I was done.

I finished every race after that out of spite and ego, definitely not skill. Those final 3.1 miles of every run I've ever completed were fueled by the vow that I would never, under any circumstances, sign up for another one of these horrible, no-good, rotten races.

For me, middles tend to be a wee bit messy, hence the name "messy middles." The excitement of beginnings may have faded, and the clarity of endings isn't yet in sight. What I've learned is that even in the tiniest of ways, hope still exists. You must seek it out and pull it into the light. Knowing that during the middle season hope retracts as the reality sets in is just one way to keep yourself on course.

Hope in the middle is less about dreaming and more about persistence. It becomes a quiet yet powerful presence that keeps us grounded. Take, for example, the story of Carlos, a school principal who found himself overwhelmed by the demands of his role. He described feeling stuck, managing daily crises while trying to maintain his long-term vision for the school. "I had to hope that my work mattered," he said as he reflected on what kept him going. By focusing on his impact on students, teachers, and the broader community, he rekindled his hope and found renewed energy to tackle these challenges.

Research in the *Journal of Management* supports this idea, showing that employees with higher levels of hope are more likely to remain engaged and resilient during periods of professional stagnation.[2] In the middle, hope often shifts from lofty aspirations to a focus on incremental progress. It reminds us that small steps add up to significant outcomes. I like to remind myself here to stick with the plan, not the feeling.

In relationships, the middle years can be a time of both deep connection and strain. The spark of early romance may give way to the realities of shared responsibilities, parenting, or navigating differences.

Hope becomes the foundation that sustains partnerships through these complexities. I recall meeting a couple who'd been married for forty-five years. They described experiencing seasons within their marriage where they felt disconnected, caught up in the routines of daily life, and even alone. Yet through intentional practices, taking the good with the not so good, and expressing gratitude, they found hope in their relationship again. "At the end of the day, all relationships have ups and downs," the husband said. "When I thought of who I wanted to do all that alongside, I would pick her every time." Hope doesn't eliminate conflict, but it does create space for renewal and growth.

Life's middle seasons often bring unforeseen challenges—health issues, career shifts, or financial setbacks. This is where hope's resiliency-building properties shine. A colleague of mine, diagnosed with multiple sclerosis in her forties, described hope as her lifeline. She didn't hope for a cure, knowing that wasn't realistic, but she hoped for strength, for moments of joy, and for the ability to continue contributing meaningfully to her family and community. Her outlook serves as a reminder that hope in the middle is about finding purpose and meaning even amid uncertainty and accepting what's in and outside of your control.

To cultivate hope in the middle seasons, focus on the progress you've made, seek support from your community, and break daunting tasks into manageable steps. Hope may not always feel bold or vibrant in the middle, but it's no less powerful. It's the quiet force that helps us endure, adapt, and stay in the race, even after mile 10.

Hopeful Endings: Finding Peace and Meaning

I read novels only with happy endings. I can handle chaos, strife, and disaster 99 percent of the way through, but on that last page she better have her happy ending, damn it! Unfortunately, I'm going to say it: Unlike in books, most endings in the real world suck. Rarely can we come upon an ending and find it simple and straightforward.

While endings are a natural part of life, they inevitably come with challenging moments to navigate. Whether we're completing a project, transitioning to a new phase of life, or approaching the later years of our journey, endings bring a mix of loss, reflection, and opportunities for processing. Hope during endings transforms from a forward-looking force into one that offers peace, meaning, and a sense of legacy.

Hopeful endings often involve letting go, which can feel bittersweet. Consider Pat, a nurse who retired after thirty-five years in the profession. While she celebrated the freedom retirement offered, she also felt a sense of grief leaving behind the patients and colleagues who'd defined so much of her life. What sustained her was the hope that her work had made a difference. She began volunteering at a local clinic, channeling her skills into a new chapter of service. While she loved the new work she'd chosen, a thread of grief was always present. "I'm getting closer to the end than I am to the beginning of my life and that's just the reality of aging," she explained. "Growing old is a double-edged sword. I've seen people who haven't had the privilege—their lives were taken too soon—but aging itself is harder than I imagined."

Research in gerontology highlights the role of hope in later life. A study in *The Journals of Gerontology* found that older adults with higher levels of hope report greater life satisfaction and emotional resiliency, even in the face of health challenges or the loss of loved ones.[3] Hope in endings helps us focus on what we've built, the relationships we've nurtured, and the lessons we've learned. While working at a local college, an instructor shared the story of one of her most unexpected students: an eighty-year-old man who had enrolled in their beauty school program, surrounded by classmates young enough to be his grandchildren. In a classroom filled with eighteen-year-olds, this senior gentleman committed himself to mastering the art of hair and makeup with remarkable precision and dedication. His attendance was consistent, and his eagerness to learn was inspiring. One day, a fellow student asked him why, at his age, he was pursuing such a course. With a steady gaze, he explained that his wife had been diagnosed with Alzheimer's disease, and she was worried that she might not be able to care for herself in the future. He wanted to ensure that when the time came, he'd be able to do her hair and makeup to ensure she maintained her dignity. "I'll always make sure you look like the classy lady you are," he promised her, regardless of the circumstances. This simple yet powerful act of hope, learning a new skill later in life with the sole purpose of caring for a loved one, embodies the extraordinary capacity for hopefilled endings.

I was asked at an event for professionals in adult assisted living communities (what we used to call "nursing homes") how to support patients or residents when the best days of their lives are behind them. The participant commented that many of them have lost hope because they're never going to get out or get better. I encouraged those who served the residents to really talk with them about their life stories. I told them that when I was visiting a facility one of the staff mentioned they had a veteran on their floor. I introduced myself to him, thanked him for his service, and asked him if he was comfortable sharing with me a fond memory about anyone he'd served with. The veteran looked pensive at first, then a full smile danced across his face and a laugh boomed through the room. "During a rainy night in France, my buddy bet me he could make a fire with just two sticks. An hour later, soaking wet, he's still at it, cursing louder than the storm. Finally, I handed him a lighter, and he declares, 'See? I told you I'd do it!' and took my money." Endings can also be a time for building legacy, as knowledge holders share priceless memories that must not be forgotten.

My dear friend Dr. James Rouse, an end-of-life doctor, is the closest person to being a true spiritual guru I've ever encountered. I'd heard of Dr. James described as a living human unicorn before I'd met him, and that descriptor wasn't wrong. He's "love and light" in human form. He often uses the expression "Thank you for showing up under the influence of love." If you imagine the purest, brightest, and gentlest feelings in the world, right up there with experiencing a newborn baby's cry and puppy breath, that's Dr. James. And he works out of a Colorado tree house! Dr. James introduced me to the idea of a beautiful death. I'd known of loss and death only as cruel and awful.

Dr. James shared with me several experiences of walking with his friends during their last moments on Earth. "I believe what's on the other side is more beautiful than anything we can even imagine. I've seen it in the moment that once-pained and cloudy eyes go completely clear in an instant with a peace, brightness, and aliveness that shifts into recognition when they see someone they're literally dying to meet." Dr. James added, "My friend looked back to me and squeezed my hand for the last time, saying, 'It's just so beautiful.'" Given that none of us are getting out of life alive, my hope for everyone I love dearly is a beautiful death and a happy reunion.

———

Clearly, hope isn't static; it evolves with us, reflecting the unique challenges and opportunities of each stage in life. In beginnings, hope is expansive and full of possibility, pushing us to dream and explore. In middles, it becomes a steady force, helping us sustain momentum and navigate the complexity of the messy middles. In endings, hope is reflective and legacy-driven, offering peace and meaning as we transition into the unknown.

By understanding how hope manifests in these seasons, we can intentionally nurture it as a tool for resiliency and well-being. Whether we're starting something new, navigating the messy middle, or finding closure at the end, hope reminds us that every moment holds potential for growth, connection, and meaning. Through hope, we don't just endure life's transitions—we embrace them, creating a lived experience that's not only bearable but deeply fulfilling.

Mapping Hope Across Your Seasons

This practice invites you to reflect on how hope has evolved in your life: how it's changed, how it's shown up (or gone missing), and what it's taught you along the way. Hope doesn't look or feel the same in every season. Sometimes it's bold and forward-facing. Other times, it's quiet and grounding. And sometimes, it's something we see only in hindsight.

Take a few minutes to reflect on an example of a major season: a beginning, a middle, or an ending in your life. You can choose experiences that were joyful, challenging, messy, or meaningful. There are no wrong choices—just honest ones.

For each season you choose to reflect on, respond to the following prompts:

1 **The season:** Was it a beginning, a middle, or an ending? An example could be starting university, parenting toddlers, retiring, moving away from home, or leaving a relationship.

2 **The experience:** What was happening at that time? Describe the moment or situation in a few sentences.

3 **Where was hope?** Was hope present in that moment or was it hard to find? Were you holding it for yourself, or did someone else hold it for you?

4   **What did hope look or feel like?** Describe how hope showed up. Was it a plan, a person, a feeling, a goal, a belief? Was it strong or flickering?

5   **What do you know about hope now because of it?** What insights or lessons about hope have stayed with you since that moment? How has your understanding of hope evolved as a result of what you went through?

Reflect on what you've learned. What did that season teach you about how hope works for you?

Why This Works

This exercise helps you make hope tangible by reflecting on how it's evolved across your lived experiences. By exploring beginnings, middles, and endings, you're engaging in a process known as narrative integration. This is a proven psychological strategy to make meaning of your past and recognize the growth that's happened along the way.

Mapping your relationship with hope through different seasons also activates self-awareness and cognitive flexibility, which are key components of resiliency. When we can look back and see where hope showed up, or how it was restored, we reinforce our belief that we have the capacity to face what's ahead, even if we don't yet know how it will unfold.

This reflection also disrupts all-or-nothing thinking. It reminds us that hope is not about always feeling optimistic; it's about noticing how we've kept going, even when we weren't sure we could. And that kind of remembering builds emotional strength, clarity, and a deeper trust in ourselves.

So whether you find yourself in a beginning full of possibility, a messy middle of complexity, or an ending marked by reflection, remember that hope doesn't disappear. It evolves. It adjusts its shape to meet you where you are. Sometimes it pushes you forward and sometimes it holds you steady. But it's always there, waiting to be noticed, nurtured, and used. Keep choosing hope, season after season. Hope doesn't expire; it adapts.

9

The Hope Blocks Model: Building a Life Tethered with Hope

> To everything there is a season, and a time to every purpose under the heaven.

ECCLESIASTES 3:1

ONE OF MY FAVORITE insights into personal growth is understanding the knowing-doing gap. Simply knowing better doesn't mean we'll do better. After all, if "should-ing" ourselves worked, we wouldn't be making the same New Year's resolutions year after year.

Every behavior serves a purpose, pushing us either toward or away from our ultimate goals. So if the goal is to bring more hope into our lives, or to strengthen the hope already there, my mission is to make success inevitable by helping you bridge the gap between knowing hope and living hopefilled in every facet of your life. I don't want you to just *know* about hope; I want you to *live* it, fully and completely. I want you to work, act, and be totally immersed in it. That's why I created the hope blocks model, a framework designed to guide you from understanding hope to embodying it. And now, for the first time ever... drumroll, please... here it is!

I'm thrilled to share it with you, and I hope you're as excited as I am.

To navigate stress, build resiliency, and achieve true well-being, we need more than just a belief in hope; we need hope practices. Through my personal and professional experiences, I've seen how these practices can transform lives. When hope is nurtured with intention, it becomes a constant, emboldening force that strengthens us even during life's darkest times.

Motivated by this, I dove deep into understanding hope, learning as much as I could to distill it into something actionable and practical so we can once again bridge the knowing-doing gap. My inner behaviorist demanded a clear action plan that could serve as a "battle board" to help you consistently show up tethered to hope. That's the hope blocks model: a structured, actionable framework designed to connect every part of your being to hope. Consider this your ultimate guide to living a life anchored in hope, no matter what challenges come your way.

The hope blocks model comprises four interconnected elements: hopefilled havens, hope-fueled habits, hope-centered work, and hope-guided self. Each block represents an essential area of life that, when forged and infused with hope, strengthens our capacity to show up in every season of our lives.

Hopefilled Havens: Spaces and Relationships That Nurture Hope

Creating hopefilled havens is the first quadrant for building a life grounded in hope. A haven is any space, physical or relational, where we feel safe, supported, and inspired. Research consistently shows that our environments play a significant role in shaping our emotional well-being. Cluttered or chaotic spaces can amplify stress, while calm and organized environments promote clarity, peace, and groundedness—all ingredients of hope. In my own life, I've found that even small adjustments, like decluttering a room or adding personal touches, can transform a space into a sanctuary where hope can flourish and grow.

Hope needs room to expand. To make room, release not just your physical clutter but the emotional noise too. I purposely start by setting up spaces and places before I focus on relationships and interactions, because I've seen how the associated behaviors—the acts of sorting, creating, and nurturing spaces—provided a magnificent return on their time investment. Puttering, sorting, purging, organizing, and completing tasks quiet the mind and help process emotions and memories. I've observed firsthand that when people's spaces are comfortable for them—determined by their own standards, not TikTok's—and they feel in control of their environment, the nervous system regulates. While we're engaged in nesting behaviors, the brain is busy healing in the background without taking in new content or repeating negative loops. Our minds also need space, without taking in new content, to process our lives in real time; keeping our bodies moving and our hands busy helps us dramatically to do this. I think of it this way: I set the table before inviting people to dinner. I need to take the time to get *me* right in my space before I invite people in, especially if I'm feeling off or dysregulated. I ground before I engage.

Another important element that ought not be overlooked is having a space or place to regulate now. It's necessary to work with your current reality. It's easy to lob the concept of haven into the future; for example, you may think, "One day I'll have a cozy and safe reading nook" or "One day I'll have my own space where I can lock my door" or "One day I'll share a home with someone who will protect me." But I need you to find just one space in your current circumstances that can serve as a refuge in this moment.

Now, havens aren't just about physical spaces; they can also be the people in our lives. Relationships are a cornerstone of our feeling that we belong and matter. Surrounding ourselves with individuals who uplift us, encourage us, and remind us of our skills, talents, and gifts creates a powerful emotional environment where hope thrives. The more we can be in alignment with our actual self, the safer and more secure we feel, which allows hope to expand. I often remind people that we're shaped by the company we keep. Investing in relationships that foster trust, kindness, and mutual support can be one of the most important actions we take in being a hopefilled person. You need a safe home team, a solid professional inner circle, and a 3 a.m. phone call. That 3 a.m. phone call is the person you can call no matter what, and they'll show up for you, even if you and your own poor choices put you into the predicament you need help in! I appreciate that for many, having these key people in your life might not be your reality, especially when it comes to family. Stepping out of dysfunction and harm, especially if it's at the hands of people who should protect you, requires finding the right support systems. Leaving and recovering from abusive relationships is possible. Blood or relationship contracts do not negate mistreatment of any kind. This is an imperative step to make room for the right people. If we keep ourselves surrounded by the wrong people, the right people won't be able to fit into our lives.

In the workplace, hopefilled havens can be cultivated through intentional design and culture. A workplace that values collaboration, encourages open communication, and fosters a sense of belonging becomes more than a place to work; it becomes a source of hope that you're part of a meaningful pursuit. I've seen firsthand how workplaces that prioritize connection, purpose, and well-being create environments where individuals can flourish, even in high-stress roles. And conversely, if we're spending most of our waking hours in situations and environments that are distress-inducing, conflictual, and toxic, we'll never be able to tap into our creativity and excellence, since most of our cognitive energy will go into managing stress, not leveling up. If you can show up for a toxic work environment forty hours per week, I beg you to show up for yourself at least an hour a day to find an exit strategy! Stay loyal to your mission and calling, not companies and job titles.

Creating a hopefilled haven requires intentionality. Whether it's rearranging your living space, nurturing supportive relationships, advocating for a positive work culture, or even leaving an unhealthy workplace, the goal is the same: to build environments where hope can take root. Negative spaces and negative people can never bring about positive outcomes. Our havens serve as the foundation for everything else we do, providing the safety and stability we need to face life's challenges.

Hope-Fueled Habits: Building Routines That Promote and Sustain Hope

Hope isn't something that just happens; it's something we cultivate through consistent, intentional actions. That's where hope-fueled habits come in. As I often say, our daily habits are the building blocks of our well-being. Tell me about your habits and I can tell you about your capacity to be resilient and the quality of your days. Habits make up our days, which ultimately make up our lives.

One of the most effective habits for fueling hope is physical movement with appropriate rest. We all know that physical activity is important for our overall health, well-being, and happiness, but there's an interesting physiological reason for this that doesn't get enough attention. Let me introduce you to hope molecules. I love these little guys! Hope molecules are a fascinating phenomenon linked to physical activity. When you move your body, whether through walking, running, or any form of exercise, your muscles release chemicals called myokines. These molecules, often referred to as "hope molecules," have profound effects on the brain, including reducing inflammation, easing stress, and boosting mood. Essentially, they act as messengers of positivity, fostering resiliency and a sense of well-being by promoting the release of endorphins and enhancing the brain's ability to process emotions. Regular physical activity isn't just a workout for your body but also a way to cultivate hope and mental strength.

Speaking of emotions, have you noticed how mental and emotional health seems to be on the decline even though we're talking about it more than ever before? Well, I have a theory about this. Our emotions aren't designed, nor have they evolved fast enough yet, to keep up with the pace of our lives. Therefore, the average person is being held back or even derailed by lingering, unprocessed emotion. Here's an example: Remember when you were a kid and had a bad day at school? On your walk home, maybe you kicked a stone, maybe you chatted with some friends, or perhaps you just looked at all the scenery around you. You weren't really acting so much as observing, just being. You likely weren't adding significant memories to the day; you were simply walking home. But without your even knowing it, these simple acts allowed your subconscious to start organizing, sorting, and processing the residual emotions from that bad day. Or perhaps you didn't walk home from school; you took a bus or had a ride. Remember passively watching the world go by or following a drop of water as it slid down the window? You didn't realize that you were like a Zen master at mindfulness by just being in the moment, watching and letting go, with your brain processing all this emotion behind the scenes.

Now fast-forward to today. Though we spend enormous amounts of time, energy, and resources trying to be mindful, I think the reason we aren't seeing the results we hope for is because we're trying to block mindfulness into segments rather than experiencing it as part of everyday moments. For example, you have a difficult meeting, and you jump into the next difficult meeting. You have a difficult task to complete, you finish it, then go into the next thing. Work has become more difficult for several reasons, one being the speed of communication and expectation of responses. Remember when information was shared in interoffice mail, those odd brown folders with people's signatures and that strange red string? Now, most information inputs come in as attachments and emails. Or better yet, once upon a time, new information was shared by the Pony Express or on the weekends when you went to the general store or to church. It took a hot minute to get updates about your neighbors and colleagues, let alone the world! Speed and access are factors on multiple fronts. Rarely do you give your emotions enough time to settle or land and be processed. The residual emotions are left just swirling around.

We also take in so much more negative content, from news headlines to polarized comment sections, and engage in disheartening digital practices like comparison on social media. And when we just jump to the next thing without processing the emotions that those headlines or the scrolling evoked, those thoughts are left unresolved. While we might practice mindfulness in a five-minute meditation or perhaps in a thirty-minute class once a week, we aren't integrating it enough into our everyday lives to allow for the spaciousness and time our brain needs to be able to process emotion.

The result of all this is an emotional health crisis. So, what hope-fueled habits help? The key to processing emotions effectively is to encourage self-awareness and emotional regulation. Each and every mindfulness practice incorporated into your day matters. Train yourself to breathe deeply before speaking or sending an email. Take time after a difficult conversation to label your emotions and process them in real time. Learn how to check in with your emotions frequently during the day without judgment. Research shows that journaling or even writing out some thoughts on sticky notes provides a space to reflect through making the invisible (your emotions) visible (written words). Physical activity, even a quick walk around the block, not only reduces stress but also helps release emotional energy stored in the body. Regular emotional check-ins, where you pause to identify and acknowledge your feelings, foster clarity and acceptance. Creative outlets like art, music, or writing can also provide a therapeutic means of expressing and processing emotions. The list of hope-fueled habits is robust. Find what works well for you and ensure that you're creating the space in your everyday life to make those habits non-negotiables.

Another aspect of hope-fueled habits is learning how to set and achieve small, achievable goals. When we break down larger aspirations into manageable steps, we create opportunities to celebrate progress. These small victories remind us of our capability and build the confidence and agency we need to tackle bigger challenges. This is also known as self-efficacy (as discussed in chapter 4), and my research shows that the best way to improve it is shockingly simple yet powerful: Do what you say you're going to do. Wild, right? The best way to improve your personal efficacy and self-esteem, which are positively associated with hope, is to set small, achievable actions and follow through.

Ultimately, hope-fueled habits are about consistency. They don't need to be elaborate or time-consuming; even the simplest actions, done regularly, can have a profound impact. My gentle invitation is to focus on building the habit first, then work to improve it. It's okay to be a rookie with a growing arsenal of hope habits. The spear is pointing in the right direction. When we weave these habits into our daily lives, they become a steady source of hope and strength, helping us navigate whatever comes our way.

Hope-Centered Work: Finding Purpose in What We Do

Work is a cornerstone of our lives, shaping not just how we spend our time but also how we view our impact on the world. If you work full-time, you likely spend more of your waking hours with colleagues, clients, or students than with your own friends and family. This reality underscores a critical truth: How we make a living and who we spend our time with profoundly influence our sense of purpose, fulfillment, and hope. In my research on resiliency, I've found that meaningful work inspires individuals to persevere through challenges, fostering not only personal growth but also a greater collective good. Hope-centered work isn't just about having a job—it's about cultivating fulfillment, building connections with the right people, and aligning our efforts with a brighter future.

To begin embracing hope-centered work, take time to reflect on what truly matters to you. Write down your core values and evaluate how your current work aligns with them. This reflection might uncover a need to pursue a new career aligned with your passions, like teaching, healthcare, or environmental advocacy. Or it might be about making small yet meaningful changes, such as initiating projects that resonate with your personal values or finding volunteer opportunities within or outside of your workplace. This alignment between values and professional efforts fosters a sense of purpose that strengthens resiliency, promotes well-being, and makes room for hope.

The concept of hope-centered work begins with aligning your professional life with your values. Studies in organizational psychology have shown that individuals who find alignment between their work and personal values report higher job satisfaction and emotional well-being. For instance, a 2025 study on psychological capital found that purpose-driven employees with high levels of psychological capital were more likely to demonstrate resiliency and sustain engagement and hope, even in high-stress environments.[1] Whether your passion is solving big challenges or creating value in smaller, everyday tasks, finding alignment with your work helps you stay motivated and hopefilled.

You can't expect yourself to be hopeful if you're spending most of your time in environments that are out of alignment with what truly matters to you, so it's imperative to identify your core values and passions. Don't just think about it: actually get specific and write down what matters most to you. Then compare this list to your current role or daily responsibilities. Consider what changes you could make to bring more alignment, whether by joining new initiatives, advocating for causes you care about within your company, or pivoting toward a career that resonates with your values.

Relationships at work are equally important in fostering hope. Positive workplace interactions create a sense of belonging, which has been linked to higher levels of motivation and overall job performance. In fact, a Gallup study on workplace engagement revealed that employees who have a best friend at work are seven times more likely to be engaged and productive and more able to stay hopeful about their futures.[2] These connections also act as a buffer during challenging times, providing emotional support and reinforcing our sense of purpose. To build these meaningful relationships, make an intentional effort to connect with colleagues. This can be as simple as initiating regular check-ins, celebrating their successes, or sharing a coffee break. Small gestures of connection often lead to stronger bonds and a more hopefilled work environment. Recognizing that these relationships aren't just professional but integral to your personal well-being reframes your time spent with coworkers as valuable and fulfilling.

Commit to building stronger connections in your workplace and notice how it changes your experience. You could start by setting a goal to have a meaningful conversation with at least one coworker each week. Celebrate their successes, offer support during challenges, and find opportunities to collaborate on projects. These efforts will foster a network of hope and motivation.

A crucial part of hope-centered work is acknowledging progress, no matter how small. Celebrating milestones reinforces the beliefs that our efforts matter and that we're making a tangible difference. This is supported by research in positive psychology, which shows that recognizing small wins boosts dopamine levels, reinforcing motivation and encouraging continued effort. Reflecting on your contributions, whether it's receiving positive feedback from a client, completing a challenging project, or simply helping a coworker, can keep you grounded in your purpose and inspired to keep moving forward. At the end of each week, set aside time to reflect on your accomplishments. Write down at least one thing you did that contributed to your goals or positively impacted someone else. Share these reflections with a trusted colleague or friend to further solidify their significance and to cultivate a sense of shared progress.

Hope-centered work isn't confined to professional pursuits. Volunteer efforts, creative projects, and caregiving are all forms of work that can be infused with hope and purpose. For instance, studies have shown that volunteering significantly enhances mental health by fostering a sense of purpose and community connection. Similarly, creative projects provide an outlet for self-expression and emotional processing, while caregiving deepens relationships and reinforces the value of love and support.

To embrace this broader definition of work, identify areas outside of your job where you can channel your energy into meaningful activities. This could include joining a local volunteer group, dedicating time to a creative hobby like writing or painting, or strengthening bonds with family through quality time and acts of service. Infusing these efforts with intention transforms them into powerful acts of hope. Choose one activity outside of work that aligns with your values and set specific goals for how you'll engage in this activity—such as volunteering once a month or spending an hour weekly on a creative hobby—and make it a regular part of your life.

By aligning your work with your values, nurturing meaningful relationships, celebrating progress, and embracing broader definitions of work, you can create a career infused with hope and purpose. Hope-centered work isn't just about professional success—it's about living with intention, resiliency, and joy in every area of your life. As Dr. James would say, thank you for showing up and working under the influence of, in our case, hope!

Hope-Guided Self: Cultivating an Inner Compass of Resiliency

The last cornerstone in the hope blocks model is the hope-guided self, your inner compass that points the way forward even when life feels like a labyrinth of uncertainty. It's truly knowing who you are, who you aren't, and who you're becoming. It's here that hope becomes deeply personal, shaping not only how you navigate challenges but also how you grow from them. Cultivating a hope-guided self begins with self-awareness. You need a good sense of all your parts, to borrow a phrase from the Internal Family Systems (IFS) model. This approach to psychotherapy views the mind as composed of different "parts," each with its own thoughts, feelings, and motivations, all guided by a core "self" that's compassionate and wise. For example, someone may have an "inner critic" part that pushes them to excel but also a "wounded child" part that carries past pain. These parts may conflict, leading to emotional distress. IFS aims to help individuals understand and harmonize these parts by connecting with the self, fostering healing and balance. So, for our hope-guided self, we need to get in agreement with all our parts!

Research in positive psychology underscores that self-awareness is a powerful driver of hope. A group of US researchers found that motivation and behavior are based on your sense of who you are (your identity); that is, you are more likely to engage in behavior that aligns with your identity—and supports your values and goals.[3] Think of it as creating your personal mission statement, a guiding star to keep you aligned when storms arise. I recall working with my very special attachment and IFS therapist and talking about how little Robyne is supersensitive, and teenage Robyne comes in ready to fight and will burn bridges like it's an Olympic sport if any part of me feels threatened. I can go from deeply compassionate and caring to "we ride at dawn, bring the heat" very quickly. The self-awareness of knowing how to work with my parts, what motivates them, and what parts I need to lean into helps me keep and protect my hope spark.

Self-compassion and self-direction are also key. Life will inevitably throw challenges at us, and knowing how we meet those challenges or setbacks matters. Instead of viewing failure as a dead end, hope thrives when we treat ourselves with kindness and see mistakes as stepping stones. Dr. Kristin Neff's groundbreaking research on self-compassion shows that being gentle with ourselves during tough times promotes emotional well-being and hope.[4] Whether you're dealing with a missed deadline, a difficult conversation, or a suspicion that you offended someone, self-compassion gives you the grace to say, "I'm human and I made a mistake, but I am *not* the mistake." This allows us to forgive ourselves and move forward. Self-compassion keeps in focus that we're innately good people who happen to drop the ball from time to time. I found the amazing Jamie Kern Lima's book *Worthy: How to Believe You Are Enough and Transform Your Life* to be a fantastic help here.

And above all else, what truly ignites the hope-guided self is embracing growth—seeing every challenge as a doorway to something greater and trusting that you're well-resourced to navigate whatever comes your way. This practice, which I like to call "light-housing," is at the heart of my research and teachings. To me, the lighthouse serves as a metaphor for combining lived experiences with research and practice, guiding us through uncharted waters by illuminating the path with the wisdom of experience, the clarity of evidence, and the stability of informed action.

Light-housing is trusting and knowing that everything we've experienced before makes us capable to show up boldly in the unknown. It's believing that our abilities can evolve, even in real time, to unlock endless possibilities we need and hope for. In this regard, nothing speaks to me as loudly as the devastating car crash

I was in when I was sixteen years old. In teaching me that I can do hard things, my mother, Lesley, saved my life. Even in unimaginable circumstances, this lesson has brought me a steadfast confidence to show up and trust that all will be well.

The hope-guided self isn't a static entity; it evolves as you evolve. It's the fusion of self-awareness, self-compassion, and a steadfast belief that you can push yourself. By truly knowing yourself, connecting with the favorite parts of yourself, and trusting that you're well-resourced no matter what, you build an unshakable inner compass, one that not only steadies you in the face of uncertainty but also inspires you to dream, grow, and keep moving forward in every season of your life. It's betting on yourself because you matter, and you have a divine destiny to fulfill.

The hope blocks model offers a practical and powerful approach to building a life anchored in real hope and purpose. By creating hopefilled havens, cultivating hope-fueled habits, pursuing hope-centered work, and nurturing a hope-guided self, we create a foundation for resiliency, strength, well-being, and growth. Hope is an active, deliberate choice that requires environments, routines, and a lifestyle that supports its growth.

Through the hope blocks model, we can forge, harness, and protect the power of hope to inspire ourselves and those around us, building a steady and bright future one block at a time.

Start Brainstorming Your Hope Blocks Blueprint

You've just explored four key areas where hope can live, breathe, and take root in your life. Now, it's time to map out what that looks like in real time for you. This quick reflective blueprint will help you translate knowledge into action and keep you tethered to hope, even when things feel uncertain or messy.

So, grab a journal, sticky notes, or a digital device—whatever feels most accessible right now. Then, answer the prompts below at your own pace.

There are no right or wrong answers here. Meet your ideas with curiosity and care, not criticism. This isn't about evaluation—it's about exploration. This is for you, designed by you, to support *you*.

Practice doesn't make perfect. Practice makes *possible*. Let's start practicing and playing with our hope blocks!

Hopefilled Havens

- What space—physical or relational—helps you feel safe, grounded, and like yourself?
- What's one simple thing you can do this week to create or improve a hopefilled haven?

Hope-Fueled Habits

- What habit currently helps you feel hopeful or grounded?
- What's one realistic, meaningful habit you can commit to cultivating or reintroducing in your day-to-day?

Hope-Centered Work

- How aligned is your current work (paid or unpaid) with your values?
- What's one small step you can take this month to bring more meaning or connection into your daily efforts?

Hope-Guided Self

- What part of yourself feels the most like "home"?
- What's one belief, phrase, or reminder that reconnects you to your truest, most resilient self?

Next Steps

Review your answers. Highlight one action from each block you'll focus on this week. Keep them visible (sticky note, phone reminder, calendar event—whatever works). This is your hope blocks blueprint in motion, and it's just a starting point. It will evolve and grow as you tend to it!

Why This Works

This exercise taps into the foundational principles of behavioral psychology, neuroscience, and emotional resiliency. By identifying small, intentional actions across four key domains—your environment, habits, purpose, and identity—you activate your sense of agency, a core driver of hope according to Dr. Snyder's hope theory. Agency is what fuels your belief that your actions matter and that you have the capacity to influence outcomes, even in uncertain circumstances.

From a neuroscience perspective, every time you complete a small, hope-driven action, you further develop neuroplasticity—the brain's ability to rewire itself through repeated experience. These repetitions strengthen the neural circuits involved in goal-setting, motivation, and emotional regulation. As you repeat these behaviors, you're also encouraging the development of the myelin sheath, the fatty insulation that helps neural signals travel faster and more efficiently. In short, you're literally building smoother, faster brain pathways that make hopeful thinking and behavior more automatic over time.

Psychologically, this process also disrupts the brain's negativity bias—our evolutionary tendency to scan for threats and dwell on what's wrong. By creating consistent micro-wins across multiple domains, you shift your mental framing from helplessness to competence. This not only builds self-efficacy (Bandura) but also increases your capacity for psychological flexibility, a key component of emotional resiliency.

When your brain begins to register success in even the smallest actions, it starts to believe, "I can handle this. I can try again. I can move forward." That's the psychological shift from surviving to actively shaping your reality. And that's the beginning of real, grounded hope.

10

Mapping Your Hope Blocks

It takes real planning to organize this kind of chaos.

MEL ODOM

I CAN SAY with absolute confidence that my life has been positively impacted by '80s television and film. I've drawn inspiration from and quoted Optimus Prime, Rocky Balboa, Indiana Jones, Bill & Ted, John Rambo, Marty McFly, Mr. Miyagi, Sarah Connor, and Colonel John "Hannibal" Smith in many of my best parenting and teaching moments. I'd be remiss not to use one of those treasured quotes here. As Hannibal Smith from *The A-Team* would say, "I love it when a plan comes together." And here, my friend, is where the plan is going to come together!

To build a sturdy bridge between understanding hope practices and actually upholding them, I've crafted key questions and templates to help you design your own hope blocks. When you do the work here, success becomes inevitable. My gentle invitation is this: Do the work if you want to see the benefit.

Thankfully, you don't need to book a week off work or wait for the "perfect" moment to begin. There's never a right time, but there is a right now! Whether you're scribbling answers on the back of a receipt, tapping on your phone, or breaking out a fancy journal, it's the act of beginning that matters. You'll find the instructions straightforward: Read the questions, answer the ones that resonate, and skip the ones that don't.

This first exercise is a primer, building insight and capacity to design your own hope blocks. Or, if you already have a sense of what fits into each block, you can jump ahead to the chart and jot down your ideas in a journal or on a blank piece of paper.

Hopefilled Havens: Define Spaces and Relationships That Nurture Hope

1 How does your living space reflect your emotional state and mindset?

2 What does an ideal place or space for processing emotions and recharging look like for you today?

3. Which sensory experiences (e.g., colors, scents, or textures) and physical items (e.g., photographs, books, or art) in your environment bring you comfort and inspiration?

4. What one action can you take to transform a room or corner into a haven of peace and inspiration?

5. How can you declutter your digital spaces, such as email or social media, to reduce stress and foster hope?

6. In what ways do the people in your life uplift or challenge your sense of hope and belonging?

7. What steps can you take to release toxic relationships and make room for supportive ones?

8. Who is your immediate go-to for support, and what makes that relationship so impactful?

9. How do your current relationships align with the person you are and aspire to be?

10. How do you protect your physical havens and your home team from the pressures of the outside world?

Hope-Fueled Habits: Build Routines That Promote and Sustain Hope

1. Which daily activities leave you feeling most energized and accomplished, and how can you ensure you do one per day as a non-negotiable?

2. What rituals can you create to make space to process emotions in real time?

3. How do you currently celebrate small victories, and how does it reinforce your sense of progress?

4. What creative outlets—art, music, or writing—help you express hope, and how can you incorporate them into your routines more?

5. What specific body-based practices help you release emotional tension or stress?

6. How do you prioritize productivity versus rest, and what adjustments could help you?

7. Which positive habits from others could you adopt or adapt into your routine?

8. How do you weave gratitude into your life, and how does it affect your outlook?

9. How can you create flexibility in your schedule while maintaining consistency?

10. What small, regular actions connect you to your core values and deepen your sense of hope?

Hope-Centered Work: Find Purpose in What You Do

1. What does success in your current role look like, and how does it connect to your sense of hope?

2. How does your work reflect your personal values, and what changes could improve that alignment?

3. Which aspects of your work feel most fulfilling, and how can you emphasize them more?

4. How do you build connections with colleagues, and how do these relationships affect your sense of purpose?

5 How does your workplace culture support or hinder your ability to stay hopeful?

6 What moments during your workday remind you of your broader purpose?

7 How do you handle challenges at work, and what strategies help you maintain hope during tough times?

8 How do you celebrate progress at work, and what does that celebration look like?

9 How can you create opportunities for professional growth that excite and inspire you?

10 How do you use your unique strengths to contribute to a larger mission?

Hope-Guided Self: Cultivate an Inner Compass of Resiliency

1 How do you define self-awareness, and how do you deepen your understanding of yourself?

2 In what ways do your inner conflicts (e.g., ambition vs. rest) impact your decisions?

3. What values guide your life, and how do you keep them central to your choices?

4. How do you practice self-compassion during failure, and how does it help you move forward?

5. Which past experiences highlight your resiliency, and how can they inspire hope now?

6. Which personal strengths have you developed over time, and how do they help you today?

7. What practices help you reconnect with purpose during times of doubt?

8. What motivates you to seek self-improvement, and how do you act on that motivation?

9. How do you integrate vulnerable or imperfect parts of yourself into your overall sense of self?

10. What specific steps can you take to bet on yourself and fulfill your unique potential?

Bringing It All Together

Next, let's use the provided templates to map your hope blocks. By writing out what's already in play, what's hindering you, and what new steps you'll take (along with the *why* and *when*), you can externalize your mental goals and make the invisible visible. Research shows that visualizing goals and mapping behaviors significantly increases follow-through by reducing cognitive load and enhancing executive function. Tools like these templates create a tangible, actionable framework to help you bridge the knowing-doing gap and build a life tethered to hope. I encourage you to let go of what you think you should write or should be doing in each block and be radically honest with yourself. You deserve to access the true insights that will make a difference for you.

These templates, also available for free on my website (see the QR code later in this chapter), are designed to help you translate your goals and ideas into tangible actions. By using the templates, you're engaging in an evidence-based process to make the invisible visible. Again, research in behavioral psychology and neuroscience supports the idea that visual representations and mapping out behaviors significantly increase the likelihood of follow-through.[1] Now, if you're even a little bit like me, you may read this chapter and think, "I'll come back to it" or "I get the idea, I don't need to write it down." My friend, you're leaving money on the table! You can't think your way through this; writing it out matters. If you really want to make the changes you haven't seen before, you may have to do something you haven't done before. Because if you do what you always do, you'll get the results you always get. Time to switch it up!

Need more evidence? A study published in *Psychological Science* suggests that visualizing goals and mapping out steps for achieving them enhances cognitive processing, making abstract ideas more concrete and actionable.[2] This is partly because visual aids engage the brain's visual cortex, linking abstract concepts with sensory input. Similarly, creating physical reminders, such as visual templates or mental cues, activates the brain's executive functions, which are responsible for decision-making, planning, and impulse control. Writing it out is how you'll level up in this area of your life. Promise!

Hopefilled Havens

Already in Play—Helps	
Already in Play—Hinders	
Going to Start Doing—Why and When	

Hope-Fueled Habits

Already in Play—Helps	
Already in Play—Hinders	
Going to Start Doing—Why and When	

Hope-Centered Work

Already in Play—Helps

Already in Play—Hinders

Going to Start Doing—
Why and When

Hope-Guided Self

Already in Play—Helps

Already in Play—Hinders

Going to Start Doing—
Why and When

Next comes the magic. I want you to pick a few words, symbols, lyrics, quotes, pictures—you name it, it's all fair game—that best reflect your overarching feeling for each block. Next, add one wild, audacious, brave goal for each block that you'll make your reality.

Hopefilled Havens	Hope-Fueled Habits
Goal:	Goal:

Hope-Centered Work	Hope-Guided Self
Goal:	Goal:

If it's easier for you to print off these charts, I invite you to download them for free from my website. You can find them at drrobyne.ca/hope or by scanning the QR code to the right!

Why This Works

This exercise taps into a powerful evidence-based strategy to bridge the gap between intention and action by externalizing your goals and making the abstract more tangible. Research consistently shows that visualizing goals and creating a clear plan for how to achieve them enhances cognitive processing, helping to transform fleeting thoughts into concrete, actionable steps. By mapping out your hope blocks—seeing what's working, identifying barriers, and planning new steps—you engage in an active process of problem-solving that significantly increases the likelihood of follow-through.

Writing it out isn't just an exercise in goal-setting—it's an exercise in making the invisible visible. Templates and visual aids help connect your goals to the physical world, activating your brain's executive functions, which are responsible for organizing, planning, and decision-making. This process doesn't just allow you to think more clearly; it helps your brain process the information in a way that leads to sustained action. Visualizing your goals alongside your current realities also reduces cognitive load, making it easier to plan and take action without feeling overwhelmed.

Psychological research supports the idea that seeing your goals and behaviors laid out visually is an effective tool for breaking down complex tasks. When you externalize your goals in this way, you're leveraging the brain's visual cortex to create more neural connections between abstract intentions and concrete steps. This method enhances both motivation and clarity by providing a framework that keeps you focused on what's most important.

The act of physically writing things down or mapping them out is more than a mere exercise—it's a crucial step in shifting from knowing what you need to do to actually doing it. While it may be tempting to skip this process or dismiss it as unnecessary, the truth is that taking this step is a significant investment in your success. As studies in behavioral psychology suggest, people who engage with tangible tools and external reminders are more likely to act in alignment with their intentions. So, by committing to this exercise, you're giving yourself the greatest chance to achieve the changes you've been hoping for.

By writing out your goals, habits, and intentions in such a concrete way, you're reinforcing the belief that you can make real change, and you're activating the momentum that will carry you forward. The act of doing this makes it so much easier to take the next step and the next, without the constant cognitive strain of trying to remember all the details. You're lowering the barrier between where you are now and where you want to go. It's time to make your hopes actionable, and this process is the best way to turn them into reality.

Ultimately, the simple act of printing or creating a visual representation of your behaviors and goals transforms an abstract intention into a concrete plan, bridging the gap between knowing and doing. See, Hannibal was right—I bet you, too, love to see a plan come together! Especially one that yields real results! And as Alan Lakein, who has no connection to the A-Team whatsoever, is attributed with saying, "Planning is bringing the future into the present so that you do something about it now."[3]

11
Gifting Hope to Others

> The smallest act of kindness is worth more than the grandest intention, for it can spark hope in the darkest moments.

ATTRIBUTED TO OSCAR WILDE

HOPE IS NOT a solitary endeavor; it's a force that connects us, lifting us collectively when we choose to nurture it in others. The reality is that we can't make someone hopeful, but we can set the stage to make being hopeful *for* that person possible. When we invest in fostering hope for those around us, whether as leaders guiding teams, families supporting loved ones, or individuals impacting society, we multiply its transformative power. Hope becomes a ripple, starting small and spreading far. In this chapter, we'll explore how to be the spark for others, with strategies rooted in science, real-world examples, and a shared belief in the potential for better days ahead.

Hopeful Leadership:
Inspiring Teams with Vision and Care

Great leaders don't just set goals; they ignite belief. Teams thrive when leaders cultivate environments where hope is both visible and tangible. Research from Gallup shows that employees who feel their work is purposeful and aligned with their values are more likely to be engaged, productive, and resilient during challenges.[1] A hopeful leader bridges the gap between where their team is and where they could be, painting a vision of success while providing the tools to get there. Take Satya Nadella, CEO of Microsoft, as an example. When he assumed leadership, the company was stuck in a cycle of stagnation. Nadella transformed Microsoft by instilling a culture of empathy and collaboration, focusing on customer-centric innovation, and driving accessibility in product development. He reoriented the company's mission to "empower every person and every organization on the planet to achieve more," aligning technological innovation with meaningful societal impact.[2] This shift not only revitalized Microsoft's internal culture but also strengthened its reputation as a trusted, forward-thinking leader in the tech industry. Nadella encouraged experimentation, acknowledged failures as learning opportunities, and communicated a clear vision of innovation. Employees not only believed in the company's future—they saw their role in building it. This alignment of vision and action is a hallmark of hope-driven leadership.

For leaders, inspiring teams is all about creating safe spaces where ideas can flourish. Psychological safety, a term popularized by Harvard researcher Amy Edmondson, is key. When people feel safe to share ideas, admit mistakes, and collaborate openly, hope grows naturally. Leaders can foster this by modeling vulnerability, such as admitting their own uncertainties while expressing confidence in the team's ability to overcome challenges. Imagine a manager who says, "I don't have all the answers, but I believe in our collective strengths to figure this out." That simple statement combines honesty with empowerment, turning a potential roadblock into an opportunity for shared hope. I'm often asked by leaders how they can be vulnerable with their teams if this doesn't feel natural for them. My gentle suggestion is to share lessons or experiences that you've already processed and resolved. I believe that people stumble on the vulnerability piece because they're talking about active situations or events that they themselves haven't figured out yet. Instead, you can share your hard-earned wisdom when you've achieved it rather than while you're still immersed in the problem. You also don't need to share all the gory details. Share only when you're ready and the lesson is harvestable.

An excellent example of vulnerability in leadership comes from Ed Catmull, co-founder of Pixar Animation Studios. Catmull openly shared with his team how, early in his management career, he struggled with perfectionism and micromanagement, which stifled creativity and innovation. He admitted that he had to learn to trust his team and embrace their ideas, even when they didn't align with his own vision. By sharing this personal growth, Catmull fostered a culture of openness and collaboration at Pixar, empowering his team to take creative risks, which became a cornerstone of the studio's success.

Other ways leaders can foster hope is by celebrating small wins to maintain momentum. When teams see progress, they build confidence for tackling larger challenges. A leader who regularly highlights milestones, whether it's completing a project phase or simply acknowledging effort, reinforces the belief that the team is on the right path. Google's Objectives and Key

Results framework, for example, emphasizes setting ambitious goals but breaking them into achievable steps, so every accomplishment feels like progress toward a larger vision. Similarly, during the development of the first iPhone, Steve Jobs celebrated every prototype improvement with his team, no matter how minor. By acknowledging these incremental advancements, Jobs kept morale high and reinforced the belief that their ambitious goal was attainable. Leaders who adopt this approach infuse hope into the process, making daunting objectives feel within reach. Another inspiring example comes from Mary Barra, CEO of General Motors, who emphasizes transparency and celebrating progress during times of uncertainty. When the company shifted its focus to electric vehicles, a challenging and ambitious pivot for the company, Barra consistently communicated small milestones to her team, such as successfully developing new battery technology or securing key partnerships. By celebrating these incremental wins, she fostered a sense of momentum and belief in the larger vision of transforming General Motors into a leader in sustainable transportation. This approach kept the team energized and hopeful, even as they navigated a highly competitive and rapidly changing industry.

Hopeful Families: Supporting Loved Ones with Compassion and Connection

Families are often the bedrock of hope, offering strength in times of uncertainty. Yet within family dynamics, hope can sometimes feel fragile, particularly when loved ones face adversity such as illness, job loss, or emotional health challenges. Fostering hope in family members isn't about offering empty reassurances; it's about being present, listening deeply, and helping them see possibilities they may have lost sight of.

I shared earlier that I felt that hope deserved a book since it saved my life. Let me tell you a wee bit more about how that came to be and who made that happen.

Despite my growing up in a loving home, some of my earliest memories are riddled with pain and rejection. I struggled with school in every possible way, both academically and socially. School hated me, and I ended up hating it right back. By the end of tenth grade, I had dropped out. The educator who'd told me in eighth grade that I wasn't smart enough to finish high school and that I was wasting every teacher's time was apparently right! I shared this recently with another former high school dropout, roughly around my age, and she recounted how her eighth-grade teacher said her only chance at a good life was to marry well! It's remarkable how a system designed to support kids can be such a central contributor to the dysfunction and pain that teenagers experience.

So, I'm officially out of school at sixteen years old, and my mental health is rapidly declining. And like many of us who need the most help, I asked for it in all the wrong ways. My cries for help took the form of addictions, self-harm, and abusive relationships—anything to feel something other than the relentless pain of my depression and intrusive thoughts. In the winter of 1996, I was institutionalized in the regional psychiatric facility. I was the youngest patient in the adult ward. The despair that took hold of my soul ripped hope from my marrow. The relentless pain gave way to a hollow numbness that stripped me of any prospect of feeling even just okay ever again. When I was asked to look ahead to tomorrow, let alone the future, I couldn't see myself there no matter how hard I tried. But thankfully, I had one person, my protector, my keeper, who happened to also be my mom, and she was not going to let me lose the fight for my life.

Because my mother, Lesley, held hope for me, I was able to commit to my recovery. When I couldn't remember what hope felt like, she reminded me. When I couldn't dream of better days, she painted me the most beautiful pictures of what she saw in my future. My mother promised me that one day I'd meet my children, who were already waiting for me to be their mom. She promised me a future was possible, and I didn't have to ever walk it alone. She assured me that I'd find my path and that she was never going to give up on me.

My mom's conviction, faith, belief in me, and unconditional love are how and why I started to recover and was able to re-tether hope into my life. At first, I was getting better for her, but then I started getting better for me. She assured me that my struggles would one day help others. "This isn't happening to you in vain, Robyne," she told me. "Your story will allow you to be of service to others. You getting better will be an example—that it's never too late, or a teenager is never too far gone, to change the course of their life. I will love you hard through all of this. You're already on your way, little one."

If a mother's love could prevent harm, hers would have shielded me from every pain in this world. But what a mother's love can do instead is foster hope in seemingly hopeless moments. A mother's love can be stronger than any grip of despair when she's patient enough to wait, holding hope on your behalf, for you to see another dawn. My mother rekindled and then protected that little pilot light within my soul. She stood up for me and boldly said no to the world when the world said my fight was over. Everything that's possible in my life today is because of how she showed up in my yesterdays.

Research on Internal Family Systems therapy highlights the importance of relational safety in fostering hope. When individuals feel secure in their relationships, knowing they're seen, valued, and supported, they're better equipped to face challenges. Dr. John M. Gottman's work on relationships underscores the value of "emotional bids," small acts of connection that build trust and resiliency over time. According to The Gottman Institute, these bids are the fundamental unit of emotional connection, and whether partners turn toward or away from them significantly influences the strength and stability of the relationship.[3]

My three favorite emotional practices for caregivers to share with their loved ones are these. The first is inspired by the great Toni Morrison and the parenting wisdom she shared on *The Oprah Winfrey Show*: "Does your face light up?" When you reunite with the people who matter most to you, let your face light up. It's a sign and ritual of welcoming each other home again. Show joy and happiness in every reunion. One day, Jaxson came home from basketball practice with a friend, and I welcomed the boys in my usual enthusiastic "This is the best part of my day, every day, seeing my kid" way. As his friend rounded the corner, he said to Jaxson, "Man, your mom is like the golden retriever of mothers. Does she always get that excited to see you?" Jaxson laughed and said, "Yes, every single time. I love what it feels like coming home." The second practice is known as the Disney hug: Always let the person you're hugging pull away first. I love how sometimes I get a quick hug from my giant teenagers and other times they linger just a wee bit longer. When I feel them wait those extra few beats, I know they're carrying something in their heart, and I know that they know I'll always be there to carry whatever I can, because they too never have to walk alone. The last practice for you here is to tell your loved ones that you believe them. When Ava comes home and tells me she had the worst day of her life at school, I tell her, "I believe you." I don't remind her of worse days she's had or the probability of something way worse happening in the future or to someone else. When someone comes in with a big feeling, believe it. Then, when they're ready, ask them whether they want comfort or solutions. It's amazing how many problems we try to solve for our kids when, really, they just want a hug. Please don't give a teenager who needs a hug a lecture.

Hopeful Societies: Building Collective Resiliency

At a societal level, spreading hope involves creating systems and communities where individuals feel empowered to make a difference. The late Desmond Tutu once said, "Hope is being able to see that there is light despite all of the darkness."[4] Societies that foster hope prioritize inclusion, equity, and opportunities for people to contribute meaningfully.

One inspiring example comes from Denmark, which is consistently ranked among the happiest countries in the world. Its societal structure prioritizes hope by ensuring access to quality education, healthcare, and social safety nets. Citizens believe that their efforts contribute to a collective good because the system supports them in return. This creates a hopeful feedback loop: When people feel secure in their basic needs, they're more likely to invest in others and envision brighter futures.

Grassroots initiatives are also powerful vehicles for spreading hope. Consider the story of Mari Copeny, also known as "Little Miss Flint." At just eight years old, Mari wrote a letter to then US President Barack Obama about the Flint water crisis. Her action led to increased national attention and tangible improvements in her community. Today, she continues to advocate for clean water and community resiliency, showing that even small voices can create waves of change. Mari's story reminds us that hope is not passive—it's a call to action.

On an individual level, contributing to societal hope doesn't require monumental gestures. Simple acts, like volunteering, mentoring, or even offering a smile to a stranger, create micro-moments of connection that ripple outward. Research from the Greater Good Science Center shows that altruism boosts not only the receiver's but also the giver's hope.[5] And other researchers found that individuals who donated money to a charitable organization activated the brain's reward pathways—similar to those triggered by pleasurable experiences like eating or listening to music.[6] Notably, these reward pathways were more strongly engaged by acts of generosity than by personal rewards. These findings suggest that altruistic behavior may significantly contribute to mental well-being and the development of social connectedness. Acts of kindness reinforce the belief that we're all interconnected and capable of making the world a little better. My dear friend Stu Saunders, the founder of The EPIC Community and the most brilliant student leadership advocate, knows a lot about the power of a micro-moment for connection. Every service person I see Stu meet, he asks them if he can tell them a joke, and his jokes are world-class. Laughs are plentiful when Stu is at the counter. One of my favorite Stu-created moments was when he had a chance encounter at a very busy Starbucks. The lines were huge, and everyone was glued to their phones, patiently waiting for their drinks. The overworked barista didn't even look up when Stu placed his order and gave the name Bradley Cooper. After several minutes, Stu waited patiently for his moment. The other barista who was calling drink names on autopilot said, "I have a blah, blah, blah [very complicated drink order] for Bradley Cooper." Stu waited. The barista repeated the very complicated drink order, but this time said,

"Bradley Cooper?" with the perfect amount of questioning lilt in her voice. Next, as if auditioning for a movie role, the barista repeated the very complicated drink order for BRADLEY COOPER. Eyes darted up from screens throughout the store as people looked around for the one and only Bradley Cooper. This isn't that crazy since they were in Vancouver, which is known as Hollywood North. When just enough people had their phones ready for that perfect shot of Bradley Cooper collecting his very complicated drink, Stu stepped forward, "That's me." And in Stu's perfect way, he sealed the moment of collective disappointment by sharing a laugh and taking a few selfies. Stu interrupted an ordinary experience by inviting strangers into a fun moment with his generous dose of humor and playfulness.

The Science of Spreading Hope

Hope, at its core, is both emotional and cognitive. Dr. Snyder's research on hope theory identifies two key components: agency (the belief that one can influence outcomes) and pathways (the ability to identify routes to achieve goals). When we help others strengthen either their sense of agency or their ability to identify pathways, we nurture their hope.

Imagine a friend facing career uncertainty. Instead of saying, "It'll work out," a more hopeful response might be "What's one step you could take today to move closer to what you want? Let's brainstorm options together." This shifts the conversation from passive reassurance to active problem-solving, reinforcing their belief in their capacity to navigate challenges.

Similarly, creating pathways for hope often involves removing barriers. For instance, a community leader advocating for better mental health services in underserved areas isn't just providing resources—they're creating pathways for individuals to access support, reinforcing the message that help is available and achievable.

The Power of Stories and Shared Narratives

I absolutely believe that stories are one of the most powerful tools for spreading hope. Narratives connect us, reminding us that we're not alone in our struggles or aspirations.

In our everyday lives, we can use storytelling to foster hope in small but meaningful ways. A leader might share a personal anecdote about overcoming a challenge to inspire their team. A parent might tell a child a bedtime story about a character who persists through difficulties to find success. Stories don't just entertain—they build bridges to possibility. I encourage you to think about the hope stories you know of, including your own, and how you can share them. I want to start a collective movement of "hope-dealers." The stories we share have the potential to radically transform lives in the most unexpected ways.

My favorite hopefilled story was gifted to me many years ago. I've since shared it on stages around the world, and I've purposely saved it for this moment.

As with most life-changing moments, the day started like any other. I was presenting at a military base to hundreds of service members. A group of soldiers shared with me that they'd recently returned home from a tour. We talked casually at first, but the conversation turned more serious. They were curious about how they could support some of their colleagues who weren't transitioning home very well. They themselves were doing all right, but other members of their division were struggling to reconnect with their family members. I asked them if they'd done anything unique or different from the others to prepare their own families for reintegration. They shook their heads and said there was nothing specific they could think of.

One soldier seemed to think a little harder, then said the group had promised that when, not if, they came home from their tour, they would finish all the household projects their wives could come up with! Another soldier said that he'd gotten half of the kitchen painted before he left. Yet another laughed and said he'd laid down most, but not all, of the hardwood floor in their living room. Each one shared a tale of some random project that they had to come home to finish.

Shortly afterward, one of the senior members and I were talking. I asked him about how soldiers and their families reconnect after long absences. The senior officer shared that every member of the military has their own approach to how they prepare and support their families before and after a deployment. I inquired about the soldiers I'd spoken to earlier, who had half-finished house projects waiting for them. This weathered and hard-faced senior officer took a deep breath and nodded knowingly. "Doc, I believe those boys leave that as a sign of hope for their loved ones that they're coming back."

I remember looking at the senior officer's mangled hands as he spoke. Broken fingers, grisly burn scars—evidence of multiple tours and trauma I can only imagine he'd experienced were in plain sight. "Robyne, when all is said and done, hope is a choice, and if you want to be of service, in whatever capacity you are called to serve, you need to find your own way to stay hopeful. No one can do that work for you."

A Collective Call to Action

As Gandalf reminds us in *The Lord of the Rings*, "All we have to decide is what to do with the time that is given us." In the time that was given to my mother, her steadfast hope for me radically changed my life. And I hope that our story, of a mother who never lost hope for her once hopeless daughter, encourages you when life feels too much. Hope isn't some distant, unattainable ideal—it's a force we can choose to cultivate, nurture, and even share with those we hold dear.

Helping others find hope is one of the most impactful actions we can take. It begins with listening, offering presence, and being a mirror that reflects their strengths. It continues with creating environments—whether in our teams, families, or societies—that make hope tangible. By modeling hope in our own lives and extending it to others, we become part of a collective movement toward brighter days.

Hope is more than a gift to be given occasionally. I believe we have a shared responsibility to one another to give it as freely and as broadly as possible. Together, as leaders, family members, and global citizens, we have the power to ensure that our lived experiences and the hard-earned lessons we've learned, especially in our darkest seasons, can become a survival guidebook for others. When we spread hope, we don't just change individual lives; we change the world.

One Hopeful Thing: A Ripple Starts with You

Hope doesn't need grand gestures—it thrives in small, consistent actions. As Gary Keller and Jay Papasan remind us in *The ONE Thing: The Surprisingly Simple Truth Behind Extraordinary Results*, by focusing on "the one thing" that matters most, individuals can trigger a domino effect where the right action, taken at the right time, leads to disproportionately positive outcomes.[7] That's just as true when it comes to hope. As a side note, for people looking to truly level up their business, this is a must read!

Look across the four hope blocks:

1 **Hopefilled havens:** the environments and relationships you cultivate

2 **Hope-fueled habits:** your rituals, rhythms, and emotional hygiene

3 **Hope-centered work:** how you contribute, lead, or support others

4 **Hope-guided self:** how you align your identity and actions with who you're becoming

Now ask yourself, "What's the ONE small thing I can do this week that would offer more hope to someone else?"

Everyday Ways to Be a Hope-Dealer for Others

Think specific, simple, and meaningful. It could be one of the following:

- Create a soft landing place for someone in your home or at work.

- Send a voice note that reminds a friend what they're capable of.

- Encourage a colleague who's quietly doing hard things.

- Ask a brave question in a meeting that others were too afraid to voice.

- Speak light into someone's story, even if just for a moment.

- Share a personal story that helps someone feel less alone.

- Gently redirect a negative conversation toward something constructive.

- Remember a big date in someone's life (anniversary, scan day, first day back) and check in.

- Offer to sit beside someone in silence—no solutions, just presence.

- Make mashed potatoes for your university student who's coming home (Hunter asks me for this every time he comes home from school).

- Advocate for someone in a room they weren't invited into.

- Leave a sticky note of encouragement on a desk, mirror, or locker.

- Include the quiet person in the conversation and make space for their voice.

- Celebrate someone's progress, not just their results.

- Hold hope for someone who's too tired to hold it for themselves.

- Protect someone's reputation in a conversation where they're being criticized.

- Reframe failure for someone who feels defeated.

- Fold a family member's laundry—apparently me folding Ava's laundry is a love language!

- Remind a friend that rest is not laziness; it's a strategy.

- Spot someone's strengths and say them out loud.

- Send a book or quote with a note: "This made me think of you. You've got this."

- Acknowledge someone's storm and say, "You don't have to weather this alone."

- Bring someone their favorite coffee or tea "just because" on a tough day.

- Make a "hope kit" for a friend—tissues, snacks, affirmations, socks, a candle, whatever feels comforting, and chocolate... don't forget the chocolate!

- Send the most "inappropriate-appropriate" meme to your friend (Thank you, Jill, Nick, and Cara).

- Give someone a mid-meeting pep talk or send words of affirmation by text message before their big presentation or interview. My friend Kim is a master of this practice!

- Share a playlist you made just for someone that lets them know you are rooting for them!

- Write a "future you" letter for someone who can't see the way forward right now. Thank you, Jay Papasan, for this idea.

- Offer to run an errand or tackle a task so someone can rest.

- Mail a handwritten postcard or letter that says, "You are not forgotten."

- Start a group chat just to celebrate someone's small daily wins.

- Save someone a seat at the table—literally or metaphorically—and let them know they belong there.

- Carry around thank you cards or just because cards, and write and give them in the moment (Kim knows the power of a perfectly timed card).

- Draw a small doodle or hope symbol and leave it where the intended recipient will find it.

- Create a hope jar with little messages of encouragement for someone to draw from when they need one the most.

- Record a sixty-second "I believe in you" video a friend can watch on repeat.

- Send an exhausted friend an e-gift card for a coffee shop (Kim's timing on sending me a Starbucks card literally saved the day while I was on an extended travel schedule).

- Buy a ticket to a talk, show, or event for someone that they would love, just to remind them life still has things to look forward to.

- Send someone a calendar invite for protected "nothing time" to rest or reset—and encourage them to take it seriously.

- Quietly step in to take pressure off someone who's struggling, without needing applause or recognition.

- Ask someone about their favorite episode of *Seinfeld* or about a Nicolas Cage movie. (My husband Jeff always smiles recounting an episode of *Seinfeld* since I've never seen one!)

- Start a tradition of "Monday morning encouragement" with someone—a single text or quote to start the week.

- Play wildly inappropriate music while driving to a basketball game to shock your baller (I have gotten Jaxson out of his head with some well-timed Drake drops).

- Take your puppy out for another walk when they thought they were all walked up for the day!

- Arrange an experience for your friend to meet their favorite '90s rockstar (for Jill, that's Gavin Rossdale).

- Practice entrepreneur Jesse Itzler's three C's: compliment generously, congratulate others, and console without hesitation.

The little things aren't really that little after all.

Pick just one. Do it within forty-eight hours. Then reflect:

"Today I was a hope-dealer. How did showing up with hope for someone else reinforce my own?"

Why This Works

This exercise taps into a powerful, multidimensional process that propels us into action. By focusing on the act of serving others, particularly in a way that provides hope, you're engaging in the same neural pathways that help you receive support. Neuroscience tells us that when we give support—whether emotional, mental, or physical—it activates the same brain regions that are involved in receiving help, including the prefrontal cortex. This part of the brain is key to emotional regulation, decision-making, and future planning, which means that by choosing to help someone else, you're actively building resilience for yourself too.

Psychologically, this exercise strengthens self-efficacy, the belief in our own ability to make a difference. When we extend hope to others, we reinforce our own capabilities and create purpose-driven actions. This sense of purpose not only deepens our sense of self-worth, but also connects us to a wider social network, strengthening our sense of belonging. Helping others to hold on to hope fosters trust, creates unity, and reminds us that we don't have to walk through life's challenges alone.

What's most remarkable, however, is the more you share hope, the more it becomes available to you. Hope isn't a finite resource—it's renewable. The simple act of helping someone else hold hope mirrors the same qualities we need to hold on to hope ourselves. Just like The ONE Thing method teaches us that focusing on what matters most leads to exponential outcomes, every small act of hope shared with others can set off a chain reaction of positive growth—for both the giver and the receiver.

12
Final Thoughts and a Parting Wish

> Success is built sequentially.
> It's one thing at a time.

GARY KELLER AND JAY PAPASAN

IMAGINE THIS: God, the Divine Architect, the Source of All Being, the Sovereign of Sovereigns, the Infinite Power that shapes existence itself, or whatever speaks to you, entrusts you with their most prized possession—a life. This life is not ordinary; it carries a mission of cosmic significance, a purpose so profound that even the heavens watch with anticipation. The decree is clear: "Take care of this life. Nurture it, protect it, and guide it to fulfill its unique purpose on Earth."

Now, everything about this life—its survival, its quality, its triumphs—rests in your hands. You are its protector, teacher, guardian, and most trusted ally. You are the architect of its dreams and the guardian of its destiny. Imagine the weight of that responsibility. What kind of life would you cultivate? What habits, virtues, and routines would you prioritize? How tirelessly would you work to keep its hopes alive and its dreams within reach? What people and communities would you allow into its world?

And now, the ultimate question: If you had to choose one set of gifts to equip this life for greatness, which would you choose?

- Set A: Followers, luck, status, looks, and an easy life.
- Set B: Family, faith, hope, love, wellness, and resiliency.

What if I told you that this sacred life entrusted to you was your own?

This thought experiment illustrates the profound value of the one life we're given. It forces us to confront the variables that truly matter. Yet society has a way of distracting us from these truths. The world whispers false promises: that status matters more than substance, that accumulation equals success, and that struggle is a sign of failure. These narratives can quietly erode our focus on what's most precious—our well-being, our purpose, and our relationships.

The Illusion of Sacrifice

Let me offer another perspective. Suppose I told you that you could have a million dollars today but would die tomorrow. Would you take it? Or what if I said you could have the money but lose your health, your memories, or your loved ones by tomorrow? Almost universally, the answer is no. We instinctively know that life, health, and connection are priceless. Yet, in the daily grind, how often do we trade pieces of ourselves—our mental and physical health, our relationships—for pursuits that ultimately feel hollow?

This disconnect often stems from societal conditioning. We're told to chase external markers of success, to never "get our hopes up," and to equate busyness with worth. Fear preys on our insecurities, and division feeds the agendas of those who benefit from our disempowerment.

Consider this staggering historical example: After World War I, as the women's suffrage movement gained momentum, a group of male doctors reportedly devised a plan to weaken the fight. They advocated for prescribing women restricted-calorie diets, reasoning that hunger would leave them too faint to protest or think critically. As Naomi Wolf writes in *The Beauty Myth*, "Dieting is the most potent political sedative in women's history."[1] Shockingly, the 1,200-calorie diet is still taught in medical schools today.

Now, pause and reflect on this manipulation. What other forces in society are subtly designed to limit our potential, to distract us from our power? Swear if you need to. (It helps you live longer!) But don't stop there—use that awareness as fuel to reclaim your focus and your hope.

As we close this journey together, I leave you with one final thought: You are the guardian of your own life. You are its protector, teacher, and champion. Treat it with the reverence it deserves. Choose the people, habits, and practices that will sustain you. Defend your dreams fiercely. And above all, never lose sight of the hope that makes everything possible.

This book has been my wee way of offering you tools, insights, and encouragement to live a resilient and hopefilled life. But the next steps are yours. Take what resonates, leave what doesn't, and craft a life that's uniquely, powerfully your own.

Remember: God, the Creator, or the Infinite Power of the Universe, whatever speaks to you, entrusted you with this one extraordinary life. You are worthy of that trust. Now go forth and live it boldly.

EPILOGUE

Do Self-Help Books Even Have Epilogues?

Do personal development books have epilogues? Probably not. Maybe this could be a first.

My favorite UK workmate (colleague to us here in North America), the one and only Phil M. Jones, has been an extremely generous and kind mentor to me. At a recent event where we both were presenting, Phil watched me from the audience. And that audience happened to be The EPIC Community led by the fabulous Stu Saunders. In attendance also happened to be my best teammate Jenna Green, my soul sister Cara Filler, my favorite co-presenter Dr. Greg Wells, my podcast co-host Peter Katz, my business bartering (à la prison style) friend Natalie Davison... just to name a few. During my presentation, in front of these brilliant and awe-inspiring humans, I said, "Hope is a strategy," to which Phil yelled, "Say it louder!" Phil—I wrote it down instead.

A Hope Manifesto

My last activity for you, dearest reader and my newest friend, is this. Read my hope manifesto below and then make it YOUR hope manifesto.

Add to it. Rewrite it. Cross out what doesn't serve you. Take it further, however you need to. Or leave it exactly as it is.

My only ask is this: Whatever you do, *live it*.

This isn't just a feel-good ending. This is a beginning.

You've walked through the science, the stories, the mess, and the meaning. You've stared down what drains you and leaned into what fuels you. You've been brave enough to tell the truth about how hard it's been and bold enough to imagine something better. Value the important stuff over your own comfort of living quietly.

This is the moment you decide what hope looks like in your hands.

Use this manifesto as a mirror, a compass, a quiet place to return to. Post it. Pocket it. Speak it out loud. Scribble in the margins. Cross out my words. Write your own. It doesn't need to be perfect. It just needs to be *yours*.

Because this has never been about knowing and memorizing what I believe. It's about remembering what *you* believe. And reclaiming that belief as your strategy for being well.

Because hope isn't soft. Hope isn't passive. Hope is not naive.

Hope is action. Hope is agency. Hope is a radical, everyday practice that keeps us well in a world that often isn't.

And now that you know that—now that you've seen it, felt it, and practiced it—hope is yours to carry forward.

Let it guide your next conversation. Let it shape your next hard day. Let it remind you what matters.

And when all else fails, let it be the spark that says:

"*I hope so.*"

Not because it sounds nice. But because it just might be the bravest, wisest, most wholehearted, faith-filled thing you could ever say.

I HOPE SO...

I believe in hope. Hope is not just an emotion—it's the force that moves me forward, even in the darkest times. It's the quiet voice that says, "Keep going," the spark that fuels my dreams, and the light that shows me a way through. Hope is my greatest strength, and I choose it boldly every single day.

Hope is my compass. Hope gives me direction. It shows me that challenges aren't the end but the beginning of something new. It transforms fear into possibility and doubt into courage. Hope keeps me anchored in the belief that no matter how difficult the path, there's always a way forward.

Hope is action. Hope isn't passive—it's a call to action. It's the decision to dream, to try, and to rise again when I fall. It pushes me to set bold goals, take small, meaningful steps, and persist with resiliency. Hope is the energy that turns my belief into reality.

Hope lives in connection. Hope is nurtured in the bonds I share with others. It thrives in relationships that uplift, encourage, and remind me I'm never alone. When I share hope with others, I create ripples of strength and possibility that inspire and unite. Together, we grow stronger.

Hope needs space. To grow, hope needs room to breathe. In spaces of calm, clarity, and intention, hope takes root. By clearing the clutter, whether physical or emotional, I make space for hope to thrive and flourish in my life.

Hope is a practice. Hope grows through small, intentional habits. Daily acts of mindfulness, movement, and gratitude build a life where hope is woven into the fabric of my being. Each habit, no matter how small, strengthens my ability to persevere and believe in what's possible.

Hope anchors my purpose. Hope connects me to what truly matters. It aligns me with my values and calls me to live with intention. Hope turns ordinary moments into opportunities for meaning, and it transforms my work, relationships, and challenges into noble pursuits.

Hope is resiliency. Hope is my strength to rise after every fall. It's the quiet resolve to trust in myself, adapt, and overcome. Hope reminds me that I can do hard things, and that every struggle is a step toward something greater.

Hope is faith. Hope is faith in action. It's the belief that even when I can't see the whole picture, something good is taking shape. Hope allows me to trust in the unseen, hold on to the promise of brighter days, and know that every step I take is guided by a greater purpose. It connects me to something bigger than myself—a force of love, grace, and possibility that sustains me through every storm. With hope as faith, I move forward with confidence, knowing I'm never alone.

Hope changes my world. Hope defies despair and sparks transformation. It's the foundation of every great movement and every quiet moment of kindness. Hope inspires me to create, dream, and believe in a better future—not just for myself, but for everyone.

This is my commitment. I will live with hope. I will act with hope. I will protect it, nurture it, and share it with the world. Hope is the force that shapes my life, empowers my community, and sparks transformation. I will stand unshaken against those who mistake hope for weakness, and I will hold hope for them, too, inviting them to see, with soft eyes and a brave heart, the quiet strength and peace of believing in better days ahead.

"I hope so…" is not the end of the story—it's the spark that writes a better one.

Acknowledgments

GRATITUDE GROUNDS US, humbles us, and connects us to the people and moments that shape our lives. How do you begin to thank those who made this book possible? One honest step at a time. So here I am, far from home, cross-legged in another Marriott hotel, laptop balanced on my knees, a cold coffee by my side, and Hans Zimmer's *Gladiator* soundtrack swelling in the background. As my teenagers would say, "Mama is in her feels." With my full heart and my misty eyes, here we go.

To the extraordinary team at Page Two—three books later, and you continue to amaze me. Trena and Jesse, your leadership is a masterclass in possibility. Kendra and Lauren—I gave you good, and you made it great. You saw the heart of my message and helped me tell it with power and authenticity. Your belief in my voice gave me the courage to go deeper and sometimes shorter! Thank you for helping me find the wisest version of my works and words to share here. And to Adrineh for her mastery of seeing the finest details and making the copy edit process seamless.

To everyone who has listened to my work—on stages, through podcasts, or on social media—thank you. To those who shared their stories, you trusted me with your dreams, fears, heartbreaks, and triumphs. You've shown me the power of words to connect us. You've reminded me that resiliency is real, and that hope can be found even in the most unexpected ways.

To my Robyne HD team—Jenna, Erin, Mikey, Katie, and the extraordinary cmi family in Calgary—you keep my professional world on axis. Jenna, an extra big thank you to you and your family. I adore you all. To my forever friends, Jillian, Alissa, Stephanie, Cara, Kim, and Nick—you are the voices on the other end of the phone and tattooed on my heart, almost literally. To my EPIC friends, Dr. Greg, Dr. James, Peter, Natalie, and Stu—being in community with you is truly epic. And to the masterful Phil M. Jones, brilliant comrade and friend, you leveled up my life and even named this book—thank you!

To my original home team—my parents, Lesley and Michael. Dad, we've shared valleys and mountaintops, and your lessons travel with me wherever I go. Mom—I am fighting the good fight for what matters most in this world: my family, my faith, and the underdogs. I have a lifetime of stories to share with you, over a cup of tea, when we are reunited. Thank you for being my *everything* in human form. And for peace of mind, knowing your prayers still protect me and your grandchildren and that Luna ran to you when her time here was done. Knowing I will see you again one day, Mom, makes my weary heart persist and is evidence you can live a wonderful life, even with a broken heart.

To my husband, Jeff—you showed up when I needed you most and never left my side. No one holds down the fort like you. I pick you every time. Thank you for being my best friend first, then my husband. And thank you for letting me be not easy to love but loved dearly, all the same.

To my March Madness Miracles—Hunter, Ava Lesley, and Jaxson—you are my greatest joy and my deepest pride.

Hunter, my protector and constant corner man, your loyalty and heart are unmatched. You stand tall for this family with courage and love. Your future is limitless, and I can't wait to watch you conquer the world. You are unstoppable. You represent everything that is good and possible. You made me a believer in unconditional love and the power of redemption.

Ava Lesley, my favorite hellcat with the biggest heart. Feisty, dedicated, wicked smart, and the one you want in your corner. You face life with courage and strength that inspire me every day. Your presence commands respect, and your smile can brighten even the darkest days. You are our one and only, and I will always be up for an Ava adventure.

Jaxson, the missing piece that made us whole. You brought joy, laughter, and hope exactly when we needed it most. Your approach to living and locking in, and your boundless imagination and effort, remind us to dream big and do it your own way. Fiercely loyal and brave beyond measure, you love and live without limits. You are one of one, destined for greatness.

Being mama to you three is my greatest blessing. Watching you love and live in this world is my proudest achievement. Take care of yourselves and each other, always. And remember—all roads lead home.

To my puppies—oh, the puppies of today and our heavenly pack! Life is better with the zoomies, snuggles, pileups, car rides, swims, snacks, and the endless joy in every reunion. Your wagging tails and bright eyes remind me that life is too short not to dive in wholeheartedly, leap into every puddle, protect the home at all costs, and chase every leaf. The chaos? That's just part of the magic. Apollo, Navy, and Memphis—you're my constant reminder to live fully in the moment, savor the fun, embrace the comfort of familiar routines, and know when to follow and when to lead.

And finally, to you, dear reader—thank you for picking up this book, especially when there are so many spicy books, funny books, scary books, and helpful books out there. And for even staying until the very last page. Of all the books in the world, you chose mine. That's not lost on me. I am forever grateful. I hope our paths cross again someday. Until next time. Take good care and be well. And be sure to *hope so*, wherever and whenever you can. Our futures are counting on it.

Sláinte!

Notes

1. Pandora's Death Jar and Robyne Thinking While Driving

1 Julie Harris, "Hope: Unraveling the Last Evil in Pandora's Box," Medium, May 21, 2023, jhwordsmith.medium.com/hope-unraveling-the-last-evil-in-pandoras-box-22f96b1d4245.

2 Friedrich Nietzsche, *Human, All Too Human: A Book for Free Spirits*, translated by Alexander Harvey (Charles H. Kerr & Co., 1908), 148. Originally published as *Menschliches, Allzumenschliches: Ein Buch für freie Geister* (Ernst Schmeitzner, 1878).

3 Theognis, Elegiac Poems 1135–50, loebclassics.com/view/theognis-elegiac_poems/1999/pb_LCL258.341.xml?readMode=recto.

4 J. R. R. Tolkien, *The Fellowship of the Ring* (HarperCollins, 2007).

5 Thich Nhat Hanh, *Peace Is Every Step: The Path of Mindfulness in Everyday Life* (Bantam, 1992).

6 Mark Manson, *Everything Is F*cked: A Book About Hope* (Harper, 2019).

7 Albert Camus, "Return to Tipasa," in *Summer* (Penguin Books, 1995).

2. Hopscotching Through Hope's History

1. Rosemarie Tong, *Feminist Thought: A More Comprehensive Introduction*, 3rd ed. (Westview Press, 2009).
2. Viktor E. Frankl, *Man's Search for Meaning* (Beacon Press, 1962).
3. Charles R. Synder, *The Psychology of Hope: You Can Get There from Here* (Free Press, 1994).
4. Frederick Douglass, "West India Emancipation," speech, August 3, 1857, Canandaigua, NY.
5. Nellie L. McClung, *In Times Like These* (McLeod & Allan, 1915).
6. Martin Luther King Jr., "I Have a Dream," speech, August 28, 1963, Washington, D.C.
7. Martin Luther King Jr., "How Long, Not Long," speech, March 31, 1968, Washington National Cathedral.
8. Nelson Mandela, *Long Walk to Freedom: The Autobiography of Nelson Mandela* (Little, Brown and Company, 1994).
9. John F. Kennedy, "Remarks of the President," speech, September 12, 1962, Rice University, Houston, TX.

3. The Costs of Hopelessness

1. Jessica D. Ribeiro, Xieyining Huang, Kathryn R. Fox, and Joseph C. Franklin, "Depression and Hopelessness as Risk Factors for Suicide Ideation, Attempts and Death: Meta-Analysis of Longitudinal Studies," *British Journal of Psychiatry* 212, no. 5 (2018): 279–86, doi.org/10.1192/bjp.2018.27.

2. Susan A. Everson-Rose and Tené T. Lewis, "Psychosocial Factors and Cardiovascular Diseases," *Annual Review of Public Health* 26 (April 2005): 469–500, doi.org/10.1146/annurev.publhealth.26.021304.144542.

3. Susan A. Everson, George A. Kaplan, Debbie E. Goldberg, Riitta Salonen, and Jukka T. Salonen, "Hopelessness and 4-Year Progression of Carotid Atherosclerosis: The Kuopio Ischemic Heart Disease Risk Factor Study," *Arteriosclerosis, Thrombosis, and Vascular Biology* 17, no. 8 (August 1997): 1490–5, doi.org/10.1161/01.ATV.17.8.1490.

4. "Understanding the Link Between Chronic Disease and Depression," National Institute of Mental Health, accessed June 22, 2025, nimh.nih.gov/health/publications/chronic-illness-mental-health.

5. Shane A. Kavanaugh, Tricia K. Neppl, and Janet N. Melby, "Economic Pressure and Depressive Symptoms: Testing the Family Stress Model from Adolescence to Adulthood," *Journal of Family Psychology* 32, no. 7 (2018): 957–65, doi.org/10.1037/fam0000462.

6. Patti Verbanas, "Maternal Depression Associated with Long-Term Economic Instability," Rutgers, The State University of New Jersey, November 17, 2021, rutgers.edu/news/maternal-depression-associated-long-term-economic-instability.

7. National Alliance for Caregiving and AARP, *Caregiving in the U.S. 2020*, May 2020, caregiving.org/research/caregiving-in-the-us/caregiving-in-the-us-2020.

8. *State of the Global Workplace Report* (Gallup Inc., 2021).

9 Sara Berg, "Half of Health Workers Report Burnout amid COVID-19," American Medical Association, July 20, 2021, ama-assn.org/practice-management/physician-health/half-health-workers-report-burnout-amid-covid-19.

10 "The 2024 NAMI Workplace Mental Health Poll," National Alliance on Mental Illness, January 2024, nami.org/support-education/publications-reports/survey-reports/the-2024-nami-workplace-mental-health-poll.

11 "Psychological Health and Safety in the Workplace—2024 Update," Mental Health Research Canada, July 2024, mhrc.ca/psychological-health-and-safety-2024; "69% of Canadian Workers Experiencing Symptoms Related to Burnout: Survey," Benefits Canada, October 4, 2024, benefitscanada.com/benefits/health-wellness/69-of-canadian-workers-experiencing-symptoms-related-to-burnout-survey.

12 Jacqueline Brassey, Erica Coe, Martin Dewhurst, Kana Enomoto, Barbara Jeffery, Renata Giarola, and Brad Herbig, "Addressing Employee Burnout: Are You Solving the Right Problem?" McKinsey Health Institute, May 27, 2022, mckinsey.com/mhi/our-insights/addressing-employee-burnout-are-you-solving-the-right-problem.

13 "The Cost of Replacing an Employee in Business," Payactiv, updated February 3, 2025, payactiv.com/blog/cost-of-replacing-an-employee.

14 "The Effects of Employee Disengagement on Company Profitability," Gallup Inc., 2020.

15 World Bank, "Hope and Economic Growth: An Analysis," *Global Economic Outlook* 46, no. 4 (2018): 32–39.

16 "Global Poll Shows People to Generally be Happy and Optimistic for 2025... yet Economic Hesitancy Remains," Gallup International Association, January 28, 2025, gallup-international.com/survey-results-and-news/survey-result/global-poll-shows-people-to-generally-be-happy-and-optimistic-for-2025-yet-economic-hesitancy-remains; UNICEF, *The Changing Childhood Project*, November 2021, unicef.org/innocenti/media/566/file/UNICEF-Global-Insight-Gallup-Changing-Childhood-Survey-Report;-English-2021.pdf. Gallup World Poll survey items used in the poll are © 2021 Gallup, Inc.

17 "How America Can Come Together Again—Robert Putnam," Harvard Kennedy School, October 19, 2020, hks.harvard.edu/centers/mrcbg/programs/growthpolicy/how-america-can-come-together-again-robert-putnam.

18 Catherine Buffington, Daniel Chapman, Emin Dinlersoz, Lucia Foster, and John Haltiwanger, "High-Frequency Data from the US Census Bureau During the COVID-19 Pandemic: Small vs. New Businesses," *Business Economics* 56, no. 3 (July 2021): 155–67, doi.org/10.1057/s11369-021-00229-0.

19 *The Lord of the Rings: The Two Towers*, directed by Peter Jackson (New Line Cinema, 2002).

4. Key Hope Theories and a Few Good News Stories

1 Viktor E. Frankl, *Man's Search for Meaning* (Beacon Press, 1962).

2 "Chilean Miners Are Rescued After 69 Days Underground," History.com, updated May 27, 2015, history.com/this-day-in-history/october-13/chilean-miners-are-rescued-after-69-days-underground.

3 Mikael Lindnord, "The Day I Met Arthur, the Dog Who Walked Through the Jungle to Stay by Me," *The Guardian*, July 20, 2016, theguardian.com/lifeandstyle/2016/jul/20/mikael-lindnord-arthur-dog-jungle-excerpt.

5. Everyday Resiliency and the Hope Variable

1 "Laughter Acts as a Stress Buffer—and Even Smiling Helps," University of Basel, July 30, 2020, unibas.ch/en/News-Events/News/Uni-Research/Laughter-acts-as-a-stress-buffer---and-even-smiling-helps.html.

2 John Baldoni, "How Humor Can Be a Leader's Friend in a Crisis," *Forbes*, March 20, 2020, forbes.com/sites/johnbaldoni/2020/03/20/how-humor-can-be-a-leaders-friend-in-a-crisis.

6. From Hope to Resiliency

1 Brené Brown, PhD, LMSW, *The Gifts of Imperfection: Let Go of Who You Think You're Supposed to Be and Embrace Who You Are* (Hazelden Publishing, 2010).

2 Margaret Irwin, Bojan Lazarevic, Derek Soled, and Andrew Adesman, "The COVID-19 Pandemic and Its Potential Enduring Impact on Children," *Current Opinion in Pediatrics* 34, no. 1 (February 2022): 107–15, doi.org/10.1097/MOP.0000000000001097.

3 Holly Mackenzie, "'I'm Bringing That Larry O to Kitchener': Murray Becomes Ninth Canadian NBA Champion," Canada Basketball, June 13, 2023, basketball.ca/news/im-bringing-that-larry-o-to-kitchener-murray-becomes-ninth-canadian-nba-champion.

4   "Quotes Falsely Attributed to Winston Churchill," International Churchill Society, January 17, 2023, winstonchurchill.org/resources/quotes/quotes-falsely-attributed.

7. Stress Wisely with a Dose of Hope

1   Ryan Klepps, "Improving Home Exercise Program Adherence in Physical Therapy," WebPT, June 20, 2018, webpt.com/blog/improving-home-exercise-program-adherence-in-physical-therapy; Rob Argent, Ailish Daly, and Brian Caulfield, "Patient Involvement with Home-Based Exercise Programs: Can Connected Health Interventions Influence Adherence?" *JMIR Mhealth Uhealth* 6, no. 3 (March 2018): e47, doi.org/10.2196/mhealth.8518.

2   Charles R. Snyder and Shane J. Lopez, eds., *Handbook of Positive Psychology* (Oxford University Press, 2002).

3   Charles R. Snyder, Kevin L. Rand, and David R. Sigmon, "Hope Theory: A Member of the Positive Psychology Family," chap. 19 in *Handbook of Positive Psychology*, ed. Charles R. Snyder and Shane J. Lopez (Oxford University Press, 2002).

4   Liz Day, Katie Hanson, John Maltby, Carmel Proctor, and Alex Wood, "Hope Uniquely Predicts Objective Academic Achievement Above Intelligence, Personality, and Previous Academic Achievement," *Journal of Research in Personality* 44, no. 4 (August 2010): 550–3, doi.org/10.1016/j.jrp.2010.05.009.

5   Rachel Domingue and Debra Mollen, "Attachment and Conflict Communication in Adult Romantic Relationships," *Journal of Social and Personal Relationships* 26, no. 5 (2009): 678–96, doi.org/10.1177/0265407509347932.

6   Nicole White, Kathleen Packard, Julie Kalkowski, and Tamicka Bradley, "Building Hopefulness Through Financial Education and Coaching," *American Journal of Lifestyle Medicine* 15, no. 1 (January/February 2021), 19–22, doi.org/10.1177/1559827620960625.

7   José Mauricio de Carvalho and Alexander Moreira-Almeida, "Existential Meaning, Spiritual Unconscious and Spirituality in Viktor Frankl," *Journal of Religion and Health* 63 (February 2024), 31–45, doi.org/10.1007/s10943-023-01902-8.

8   Nelson Mandela, *Long Walk to Freedom: The Autobiography of Nelson Mandela* (Little, Brown and Company, 1994).

9   Stephen Hawking, speech, Oxford Union, November 15, 2016, Oxford, UK, hawking.org.uk/in-words/speeches/speech-5.

8. The Evolution of Hope Across Life's Seasons

1   Benjamin Mee, *We Bought a Zoo: The Amazing True Story of a Young Family, a Broken Down Zoo, and the 200 Wild Animals That Change Their Lives Forever* (Weinstein Books, 2008).

2   Carolyn M. Youssef and Fred Luthans, "Positive Organizational Behavior in the Workplace: The Impact of Hope, Optimism, and Resilience," *Journal of Management* 33, no. 5 (October 2007): 774–800, doi.org/10.1177/0149206307305562.

3   Miles G. Taylor and Dawn Carr, "Psychological Resiliency and Health Among Older Adults: A Comparison of Personal Resources," *The Journals of Gerontology: Series B* 76, no. 6 (July 2021): 1241–50, doi.org/10.1093/geronb/gbaa116.

9. The Hope Blocks Model

1. Eka D. Aprilia, Muhammad Adam, Zulkarnain Zulkarnain, and Marty Mawarpury, "The Role of Psychological Capital and Meaningful Work in Enhancing Well-Being," *SA Journal of Human Resource Management* 23 (May 27, 2025): a2984, doi.org/10.4102/sajhrm.v23i0.2984.

2. Jim Collison, host, *The CliftonStrengths Podcast*, webcast, "Why Having a Best Friend at Work Is Important," Gallup, December 5, 2022, gallup.com/cliftonstrengths/en/406298/why-having-best-friend-work-important.aspx.

3. Daphna Oyserman, Neil A. Lewis Jr., Veronica X. Yan, Oliver Fisher, S. Casey O'Donnell, and Eric Horowitz, "An Identity-Based Motivation Framework for Self-Regulation," *Psychological Inquiry* 28, no. 2-3 (2017): 139-47, doi.org/10.1080/1047840X.2017.1337406.

4. Kristin Neff, "Self-Compassion and Psychological Well-Being," *Constructivism in the Human Sciences* 9, no. 2 (2004): 27-37.

10. Mapping Your Hope Blocks

1. Lace M. Padilla, Sarah H. Creem-Regehr, Mary Hegarty, Jeanine K. Stefanucci, "Decision Making with Visualizations: A Cognitive Framework Across Disciplines," *Cognitive Research: Principles and Implications* 3, no. 1 (December 2018): doi.org/10.1186/s41235-018-0120-9.

2. Jooyoung Park, Fang-Chi Lu, and William M. Hedgcock, "Relative Effects of Forward and Backward Planning on Goal Pursuit," *Psychological Science* 28, no. 11 (November 2017): 1620-30, doi.org/10.1177/0956797617715510.

3 BrainyQuote, "Alan Lakein Quotes," accessed May 29, 2025, brainyquote.com/quotes/alan_lakein_154655.

11. Gifting Hope to Others

1 Jim Harter and Ben Wigert, "The Post-Pandemic Workplace: The Experiment Continues," Gallup Inc., March 11, 2025, gallup.com/workplace/657629/post-pandemic-workplace-experiment-continues.aspx.

2 Satya Nadella, "What Empowerment Means to Us," Microsoft, accessed May 29, 2025, news.microsoft.com/empowerment.

3 Ellie Lisitsa, "An Introduction to Emotional Bids and Trust," The Gottman Institute, accessed June 27, 2025, gottman.com/blog/an-introduction-to-emotional-bids-and-trust.

4 President of the 76th Session of the General Assembly of the United Nations, speech at the memorial service for Archbishop Desmond Tutu, Cathedral of St. John the Divine, New York, NY, February 13, 2022, un.org/pga/76/2022/02/13/memorial-service-for-archbishop-desmond-tutu.

5 Hope Reese, "Can Altruism Help Us Through Hard Times?" *Greater Good Magazine*, June 10, 2025, greatergood.berkeley.edu/article/item/can_altruism_help_us_through_hard_times.

6 Jorge Moll, Frank Krueger, Roland Zahn, Matteo Pardini, Ricardo de Oliveira-Souza, and Jordan Grafman, "Human Fronto-Mesolimbic Networks Guide Decisions About Charitable Donation," *Proceedings of the National Academy of Sciences of the United States of America* 103, no. 42 (October 17, 2006): 15623–8, doi.org/10.1073/pnas.0604475103.

7   Gary Keller and Jay Papasan, *The ONE Thing: The Surprisingly Simple Truth Behind Extraordinary Results* (Bard Press, 2013).

12. Final Thoughts and a Parting Wish

1   Naomi Wolf, *The Beauty Myth: How Images of Beauty Are Used Against Women* (William Morrow & Co., 1991), 187.

Josie Cipriano Photography

About the Author

DR. ROBYNE HANLEY-DAFOE is on a mission to make life's toughest challenges not just manageable but meaningful. Described as the "friendly neighborhood scientist" who makes the complex refreshingly simple and relatable, Dr. Robyne blends cutting-edge research with real-life wisdom to teach resiliency, stress navigation, and optimal performance—all with a dash of humor and a whole lot of hope and heart.

An award-winning behavioral educator, Dr. Robyne earned the 2022 Silver Nautilus Award for Psychology/Mental & Emotional Well-Being for her debut book *Calm Within the Storm: A Pathway to Everyday Resiliency*, placing her among the world's leading voices on human resiliency. Her second book, *Stress Wisely: How to Be Well in an Unwell World*, won the 2023 Silver Award in Self-Help from the IBPA Benjamin Franklin

Awards, the 2023 Bronze Award for Self-Help by the Foreword INDIES Book of the Year Awards, and the Grand Prize in the BookLife Prize Nonfiction Contest.

At home in Central Ontario with her husband Jeff, Dr. Robyne is a proud mom to three extraordinary teenagers—Hunter, Ava Lesley, and Jaxson—who keep her humble, hungry, and hilariously grounded. Fueled by coffee, historical fiction, her puppies, and the elusive dream of a spotless kitchen, she navigates motherhood and career with the same resiliency and hope she teaches.

Dr. Robyne's mission is bold and simple: to prove that hope is a strategy, resiliency is a skill, and better days are always within reach.

Work with Dr. Robyne Hanley-Dafoe

Dr. Robyne and her team are committed to helping people find their own path for carrying the weight of the hard parts of their lives. We embolden and empower people through our sharing of practical, research-informed strategies and community. We strive to break down barriers so people can live truly well. We believe that each and every person can do hard things and great things.

Be sure to follow us on social media and sign up for our newsletter!

- @dr_robynehd
- drrobynehd
- drrobyne.ca

Together, we will explore the challenges that humanize us all. There is a place for you here.

Dr. Robyne is available for keynotes, consultation, coaching, training, and professional development opportunities ranging from one-on-one to company-wide initiatives.

Learn more about Dr. Robyne's innovative programs, including cutting-edge open educational resources, engaging online courses, and supplementary book tools, including a free book club guide, at drrobyne.ca.